E.ASIA

FOODS of the ORIENT

SOUTH-EAST ASIA

Introduced by Sharmini Tiruchelvam

ENIGMA

Picture Credits

Alan Duns	14, 37, 64, 75, 84, 96
Garner/AAA Photos	10
Burt Glinn/Magnum	7
Paul Kemp	22
David Levin	69
Roger Phillips	18, 28, 34(B), 43/44, 48
	51, 58, 63, 72, 79, 89,
	93, 98
Iain Reid	34(T)
Raghubir Singh/J. Hillelson	6, 9
David Smith	78
George Wright	38

Edited by Isabel Moore
and Jonnie Godfrey

Published by Marshall Cavendish Books Limited
58 Old Compton Street
London W1V 5PA

© Marshall Cavendish Limited 1978, 1979

First printing 1978
Second printing 1979

Printed in Great Britain

ISBN 0 85685 481 6

CONTENTS

INTRODUCTION TO SOUTH EAST ASIA

Sharmini Tiruchelvam

It has been said that all South-East Asian cooking is essentially peripheral to the cuisine of China. True – yet not quite true. The influence is certainly there: Singapore, Malaysia and Indonesia contain large immigrant Chinese populations which retain their traditional styles of cooking, undoubtedly influencing the cuisine of these countries, and both Vietnam and Burma became vassal states of China in the reign of the Emperor Chien-lung, with consequent effects on both culture and gastronomy. Despite this, however, the cuisines of Malaysia, Indonesia, Thailand and Burma (which together with those of Singapore, Vietnam, the Philippines and Cambodia are commonly and collectively called South-East Asian) remain more accurately and essentially based on the cuisine of India, on its methods and styles of cooking and types of dishes.

There are the hot spiced gravy dishes called *gulehs* or *kares* or curries, similar to the curries of South India, although usually much less spicy and hot. The custom in Indonesia, Burma and Thailand of having savoury-soupy accompaniments to some of their rice meals again resembles that of South India with its *rasams* and *mulligatawnies*. The *sambals* are very like the Indians' too: piquant hot mixtures, with chilli always present in some form or other, and in South-East Asia invariably combined with prawn or shrimp paste (*blachan*). As with the Indians, sambals are served both as appetizers and as an integral part of the main meal, and in South-East Asia the idea has been further refined to make *sambals goreng* dishes in which sambal sauces are combined with other ingredients (herbs, spices, sugar and thick coconut milk) and fried with meat, fish or vegetables.

The *rendangs* of the Malays are obviously derived from the great 'dry' curries of India although, again, made much less hot and marginally sweeter with the addition of ingredients such as jaggery (raw sugar) or a sweet fruit. The Malays also have a mild, thick-gravied meat dish which they call *korma*, which is patently one form of the Indians' classic range of the same name.

From the Chinese, though, comes one of the most popular forms of cooking: stir-frying in a wok. And, from them, too, the art of tossing together unusual assortments of fresh and dried meats, fresh, preserved and dried seafood, fresh and preserved vegetables, herbs, spices and flavourings, in apparently numberless computations of combinations. The mixing of several kinds of meat and seafood within the same dish is so popular here that it is now widely regarded as a typically South-East Asian trait!

When a blander dish is absorbed from another cuisine – especially the Chinese – it is invariably adapted to the local taste by being 'hotted' up either by being combined with a spicy sauce, or by being accompanied by a hot or piquant dip. *Poppia*, that inspired Malaysian snack, is a perfect example: a version of the much simpler Chinese spring roll, it is made of diced ban quan (Chinese turnip), cooked shrimps, shredded crab and chicken, uncooked fresh bean sprouts, tiny cubes of fried bean curd, crisp-fried and cubed pork fat, dried prawns (shrimp), all wrapped up in fresh lettuce leaves, then in wafer-thin white pancakes, or fried crisp within a thin, light pastry. *Poppia* has two important points to it: first, the combination of fresh and dried versions of some of the same ingredients and, second, a smear of hot *blachan* (shrimp paste) within the pancake. This seems not only to give the whole dish a 'kick' but also to combine all the other mouth-watering flavours more successfully.

There are certain herbs, grasses, leaves, roots, fruits, seeds, nuts and dried preparations which are an essential part of the cooking and flavours of the region: lemon grass, daun pandan, laos, blachan, celery, cumin, coriander and coriander leaf (Chinese parsley), cloves, cardamoms, green ginger, fennel, curry leaves, sesame seed, sesame oil, limes and lemons, mustard seeds (whole or bruised but not powdered), whole nutmeg (grated freshly just before use), bean sprouts, black bean sauce, soy beans, soy sauce, bean curd, lotus seeds, water chestnuts, Chinese mushrooms, spring onion (scallions), tamarind, turmeric, peppers – green and red, dried squid, dried scallop cakes, dried prawns and shrimps, the list is exotic – and endless. Yet you can manage with only a few really indispensable ones, plus some inspired substitution! Which is how, in fact, many of the cuisines of the area were created.

All the lands of South-East Asia have access to the sea; all have therefore a great range of seafood at their disposal – the cooking of which they are all expert. Great attention is paid to what fish is in 'season'. What will cook best in what manner – What is best sautéed? . . . What steams or stir-fries

best? . . . What is best curried or devilled? – are all important questions. Mackerel does not steam well whereas it will sauté beautifully, sea bass and turbot are delicious steamed; pike poaches well; bream and red mullet both sauté and fry well. All are recognized and the most of them made. Fish-based soups and bouillons are popular especially in Burma, Thailand and Indonesia.

Like the Chinese, the South-East Asian cook pays very great attention to the quality and intrinsic properties of the ingredients; knowing what will combine most successfully with what is considered to be of paramount importance. Which leads to another very important aspect of South-East Asian cooking: it is not only the knowledge of these qualities but having the skill to choose the best raw materials that is important. It is, in fact, the starting point for much of the cooking. Many rules, handed down for generations by word of mouth within families, exist side by side with regional folklore.

Some foods are considered more healthy and 'cooling', others rich and/or 'heaty'. Like the Yin and Yang of the Chinese: 'heaty' and 'cooling' balancing opposites. One must learn how to combine them within a meal. Crabs, lobsters and oysters, for example, are heaty foods, as is garlic: they inflame the body and the passions, they say. White marrow (squash), lettuce, cucumber and milk are cooling. Pineapples and mangoes are heaty whereas limes and lemons are cooling. Yams and potatoes are heaty. Durian inflames; mangosteens

cool. It is always wise to follow a meal of the former group with a balancing amount of the latter. Many of the injunctions turn out to be surprisingly accurate. Drink milk or water out of the shell of the durian whose flesh you have eaten and you will not have any durian breath – a social disaster far worse than garlic breath. It is true! And . . . never buy crabs which have been caught in the waning season of the moon. The flesh is full and firm only when the moon is waxing, they say. Astonishingly, again, this too turns out to be true. The shells are a quarter or more filled with liquid and the flesh rather soft. But once the rules for the selection of the raw materials and the combination of the ingredients have been observed, along with the basic rules of health and hygiene, the rest is wide open to invention and innovation. In short, they are culinarily adventurous.

Derived then from the two great cuisines of the East – Indian and Chinese – influenced early by the trader Arabs and the Polynesians, linked together later still by invading foreigners from the West – the Portuguese, Dutch and English – South-East Asian cooking is not so much a great cuisine as it is a no-holds-barred amalgam of many cuisines.

There is no doubt that there is a strong regional similarity, especially between countries like Malaysia and Indonesia, Burma and Thailand. Indeed there is a great regional link, based on similar geography and climate – with access to the same food-rich terrain, oceans, seas and rivers. Common historical and ethnic bonds further bind them.

the development of the Malaysian (and Indonesian) cuisine. Undoubtedly it is descended from the trader Arabs' kebab, yet it has been developed into such a unique culinary item as to merit being classified as a classic dish in its own right. The Malaysian and Indonesian sate is made from sliver-thin pieces of beef, veal, lamb, poultry of any kind, livers, tripe (or even pork – this usually being cooked by the Chinese, pork being taboo to the Muslim Malay). These are first marinated in a sauce before being skewered and barbecued. Cooked correctly, sate should melt in the mouth. It is served straight off the fire on the skewers on which it was cooked, together with pieces of raw onions and cucumber cubes (thereby correctly balancing the overall dish) and a hot, cooked sate sauce, with a base of chillis and ground roasted peanuts (or peanut butter). It makes a marvellous first course to a meal.

The Chinese: In many of the South-East Asian cities, and especially in Singapore and Malaysia, there are whole streets of restaurants and mobile kitchens (stalls) which specialize in the cooking of any one of the separate regions or schools of Chinese cooking such as Peking (Shantung), Honan, Hunan, Fukien, Schezwan, Yang Chow, Hokien and, of course, Canton. In the final analysis, however, there are really three main types of Chinese cooking in South-East Asia: the haute cuisine of China as practised by the chefs in the restaurants; the provincial and regional home-cooking of China as made every day in the homes of the Chinese, and the Malaysian-Chinese cooking which has been evolving over the past century since the arrival of the immigrant Chinese coolie population within the Malay Archipelago.

All Malaysian-Chinese dishes have been adapted from the Chinese with a couple of exceptions such as pork or tripe sate taken from the Malays and dishes like curry mee taken from the Indians. Very popular dishes in this range too, are mah mi, quay thiau and mi hoon – which are made goreng, rubus or soto – i.e. fried, boiled or soupy.

Quay Thiau Goreng, for example, is a sort of tagliatelle al vongole, made with clams, eggs, flat noodles, bean sprouts, a soupçon of chilli powder, garlic, onion (optional), salt and soy sauce stir-fried in a wok. In a very grand version of this one you could use oysters! Perak, in North-Central Malaysia is supposed to make the best quay thiau. And one little man with a mobile stall, in Ipoh, called 'the Spider' makes it so well, with clams, that gourmets from all over the East, from princes to poor men, come to eat nightly at his stall.

Poppia has already been described. Lobak is a sort of tempura: soft-shelled baby crabs, crayfish, baby lobsters, giant prawns (shrimps) in their shell, squid, peppers and certain yams and a marvellous Chinese sausage are all dipped into the lightest of batters and crisp-fried, so that it is possible to eat

Despite all that, however, the cooking of each of the different countries is today quite distinct. Gourmets and experts on the cooking of the region can easily differentiate between the same dish cooked in the styles of two different countries: they can say, for example, if it is an Indonesian or Malaysian rendang merely by smelling it . . . So they say!

Malaysia and Singapore

There are four main groups of people in Malaysia and Singapore: the indigenous Malays, the immigrant Chinese, the once itinerant trader Indians and Sri Lankans, the former invader Europeans . . . . What is most important about the various groups is the fact that they all still keep to their own traditional styles of cooking, adding greatly to the local repertoire, even as they have adapted their own palates – religious taboos allowing in some instances – to appreciate a wide variety of other ethnic foods.

The Malays: Malaysian cooking is like that of their close relatives, the Indonesians, and has evolved most directly from the availability of foodstuffs locally, combined with the outside influence of the trader Arabs bringing in the spices of the Indians. Finally when the Indians themselves settled in their midst they were greatly influenced by that cuisine and from the names of their dishes alone one can trace the links (many of them shared with the Indonesians): rendangs, gulehs, ajars, sambals, sambals goreng.

Sate (or satay in Malaysia) is a good example of

the whole crab or prawn without having to spit out the shell. *Yong thou foo* is another delicacy, made with peppers, seeded red chillis, aubergines (egg-plants), marrows (squash), bitter gourds and bean curd cakes all stuffed with quenelles of pounded fresh fish or pork with onions, garlic and herbs and cooked for a very few minutes in simmering, delicate fish broth.

These Malaysian-Chinese dishes are made particularly well by the stall and mobile kitchen cooks. Throughout the whole of South-East Asia there is the phenomenon of the nocturnal cities and towns. Hundreds of thousands of mobile kitchens and stalls (each usually specializing in one or two dishes) mushroom even in the residential districts around the towns after sundown, and keep going until about midnight. Their expertise is hard to equal.

In Malaysia, especially in Malacca and Penang where the races intermarried more than on the mainland, there developed yet another strain of cooking primarily derived from the Chinese, but clearly and equally mixed with Indian and Malay cooking. Nowadays, it is called Straits Chinese or *nonya* cooking and there is great interest in it, especially in Singapore. The cuisine evolved when many of the Chinese men who came to these areas, well-off and ambitious traders who did not bring their own women, married the local Indian and Malay women (called *nonya* – hence the name of the cuisine). These men lived like princes and ate even better . . . for their foreign wives, wanting to please them, learned how to prepare their native dishes but invariably adapted them to their own tastes and local availability.

The Indians and Sri Lankans: As with the Chinese, there are as many different sects and groups of Indians and Sri Lankans here as there are to be found on their mainland – Punjabis, Bengalis, Gujeratis, Sindhis, Telugus, Nepalese, Pathans, Kashmiris, Goans, Tamils, Singhalese – and each continues to practise its own regional and classic cooking. But undoubtedly the greatest influence has been that of the South Indians, most specifically the Indian Tamils.

Indonesia
The cuisine of Indonesia is very similar to that of Malaysia, having basic ethnic, geographical, cultural, historical and religious links, and also having been influenced in turn by the Arabs, the Indians and the Chinese – each bringing their own culinary customs and religious taboos. More particularly, however, Indonesia's cuisine must be described as having been formed out of the cuisine of what was once Java and Sumatra.

The Javanese and Sumatrans: Javanese cuisine is based on the availability of local produce, the fruit of a fertile land tended by a fairly well popu-lated and highly agricultural community. Everything is used very fresh and according to season, and the

dishes, although sometimes quite sophisticated, contain fewer Indian spices than Sumatra, which was more exposed to the Arab and Indian trader traffic. Instead, the Javanese use more sugar (which grows there), and much trasi (dried shrimp paste).

The Sumatrans, early exposed to Islamic traders, soon adapted their cuisine to the use of the imported spices: fennel, cumin, coriander, chilli, ginger, cardamoms, cinnamon, so that it was recognizably different from that of Java with its sweeter, trasi-flavoured dishes. They also use more chillis and ginger than the Javanese. In central Sumatra, where a very orthodox form of Islam is practised, meat and fish are prepared in a very austere way; in contrast to Central Java where there is a great light-heartedness – much more truly South-East Asian!

The Dutch: There is some confusion, especially in Western minds, about the influence of the Dutch on Indonesian cooking. It is believed that they *invented* Rijsttafel. Certainly the word is Dutch, (it means, literally translated, rice table). But it is not a dish but the description of a table set at once with about 30–40 dishes ranging from complex meat, fish and vegetable curries, sates, rendangs, soups, sambals, ajars, gado-gados and other accompani-ments. In short it is a table holding practically all the various famous Indonesian and Indian dishes of that area, in quantities to enable everyone to have a bit of everything. The Dutch loved eating it! The basis is usually a great dish of exquisite, plain white boiled rice, although a saffron or turmeric flavoured rice is sometimes served. The average Indonesian meal consists of the classic combination of chicken, meat, fish, vegetable and egg dishes together with a savoury soup, various sambals, ajars, etc. There are usually about eight accompanying dishes to the basic rice of the meal.

Thailand
Although geographically closer to Malaysia, by some curious quirk Thai food is remarkably similar to that of Java! Like most Indonesians and unlike most Malays, they invariably serve a soup with their rice meals. And like the Javanese they use chillis, sugar, garlic, blachan and laos powder. Like the Indonesians, too, they decorate their food won-derously.

Thailand is a particularly excellent example of the dual heritage from India and China. For an average Thai meal will have, if rice based, a savoury soup eaten with the rice as the Southern Indians do, a curry or two and one or two obviously Chinese dishes only slightly modified to the South-East Asian taste.

The herb for which they have a passion is coriander leaf, and it is sprinkled liberally over almost every dish in the cuisine. They also use a great deal of crushed garlic and coriander root –

which is very much an acquired taste. *Nam pla* is a pungent fish sauce which is used greatly as a base in their cooking and *nam prik* is a hot fish sauce which is found on every Thai table – like soy sauce at a Chinese meal! It is used with everything except the sweet . . . .

Lahp Isan is a sort of Northern Thai spiced and savoury steak tartare. Java has Gado-Gado and Malaysia Rojak and so, too, in Thailand are *Yam Chomphu* a tart fruit salad, flavoured with fish sauce, tamarind or lemon-water, and sugar, *Yam Taong* and *Som Tom* the former with cooked shrimps, pork, crabmeat and dried shrimp with vegetables, the latter with mixed vegetables only. In Thailand, fish sauce replaces the Indonesian blachan-peanut-chilli sauce.

Burma

Once again the two parent cuisines are recognizable, but combined here in a typically Burmese way. In their daily life the Burmese have dishes which, like the Thais, clearly shows them to have a cuisine which is an amalgam of both the Indian and Chinese cuisines seafood and fish gravies dominate. Soups like *Hincho* with a fish gravy base, courgettes (zucchini) and cabbage and *Nga Hin*, again with a fish gravy base, fish, oil, sugar, tomatoes, onions and garlic are much loved. Each person usually has a bowl of soup with the rice-based meal. Mutton, especially, and beef are cooked with more spices than fish or poultry. Pork dishes are usually cooked Chinese-style. Shrimps fried with onions, garlic, ginger, chillis and a dash of sugar summarizes the South-East Asian cooking story here.

Vietnam and Cambodia

Vietnam and Cambodia have a cuisine which has been chiefly derived from the Chinese but greatly influenced by the presence of the French in their midst. Both have 'hot' dishes, which they call curries, but which owe more to Burma than to India, and which are served with noodles as often as with rice. Both have a passion for fish sauce – the Vietnamese version is heavier and saltier than anywhere else and is used not only in cooking but, diluted (called *nuoc cham*), as a garnish over almost everything!

The Philippines

The islands of the Philippines are rather an anomaly in South-East Asia, for here the influence is as much Spanish and American as Indian and Chinese, and both living and eating styles reflect this. The most popular stew, made with pork, or pork and chicken, is called *adobo*, and there is a version of that perennial Spanish favourite *arroz con pollo*. But the Chinese and Malay-Chinese influence *is* there, in a national snack called *lumpia* (a sort of spring roll), in

pancit molo (a sort of wonton soup) and a fondness for cooking in coconut milk.

Garnishes
South-East Asians have great grace and talent in garnishing their food, even the simplest daily meal. They use their natural materials – especially their fruit and vegetables – with considerable awareness of colour and texture. It is an art at which they all seem to be naturally adept: making lotuses out of onions, wild lilies out of carrots and chillis, crysanthemums out of papayas, roses from tomatoes, sea-anemones out of mangoes and melons, radish carnations, and Birds of Paradise out of pineapples and assortments of other fruits and vegetables, with an apparent ease as to make a sculptor swoon with envy.

There is one more quality common to all the countries of South-East Asia: a marvellous regional spirit. It pervades everything, not least their food. The ritual and enjoyable aspects of eating and serving food is very much to the taste and nature of the South-East Asian, the 'ritual' being of a Polynesian hedonistic sort rather than that of the courtly sophistication or religious traditions of the Chinese and Indians.

The very breaking open of crabs, lobsters or crayfish at the table; the breaking open and assessing of the first fruit of the seasons; the informality of using one's fingers; the creative delight of 'orchestrating' one's meal, dipping in at will, into the several flavours of the accompanying sauces and dips; the generous ceremonies of sharing and eating together, invariably informally and very relaxed, has a marvellous sensual sense of the sheer daily celebration of life . . . .

Since time immemorial the junk has plied the seas of the Orient, transporting everything from food to people. Even in modern times its popularity remains undiminished – the picture left shows a present day version entering Singapore harbour, its cargo of fish destined for the markets there.

11

SOUPS

SINIGANG

(Fish Soup)   (Philippines)

Metric/Imperial	American
400g./14oz. tin tomatoes	14oz. can tomatoes
2 onions, finely chopped	2 onions, finely chopped
1 large sweet potato, peeled and cut into cubes	1 large sweet potato, peeled and cut into cubes
225g./8oz. spinach, chopped	$1\frac{1}{3}$ cups chopped spinach
1 Tbs. tamarind pulp (optional)	1 Tbs. tamarind pulp (optional)
1.2l./2 pints water	5 cups water
salt and pepper	salt and pepper
$\frac{1}{2}$kg./1lb. firm white fish fillets, chopped	1lb. firm white fish fillets, chopped

Put the tomatoes and liquid, onions, vegetables and tamarind into a large saucepan. Pour over the water and seasoning to taste and bring to the boil. Reduce the heat to low and simmer for 15 minutes. Stir in the fish fillets and simmer for a further 15 to 20 minutes, or until the fish flakes easily. Serve at once.
Serves 6
Preparation and cooking time: 45 minutes

TOM YAM KUNG

(Shrimp and Lemon Soup)   (Thailand)

Metric/Imperial	American
1kg./2lb. prawn in the shell	2lb. shrimp in the shell
1.75l./3 pints water	$1\frac{1}{2}$ quarts water
2 tsp. chopped lemon grass or grated lemon rind	2 tsp. chopped lemon grass or grated lemon rind
$\frac{1}{4}$ tsp. ground ginger	$\frac{1}{4}$ tsp. ground ginger
3 lemon, lime or other citrus leaves (optional)	3 lemon, lime or other citrus leaves (optional)
2 dried whole chillis	2 dried whole chillis
1 Tbs. fish sauce	1 Tbs. fish sauce
2 Tbs. lemon juice	2 Tbs. lemon juice
1 red chilli, finely chopped	1 red chilli, finely chopped
3 spring onions, chopped	3 scallions, chopped
2 Tbs. chopped coriander leaves	2 Tbs. chopped coriander leaves

Shell and devein the prawns (shrimp) setting aside the meat. Put the shells and heads into a large saucepan and pour over the water. Stir in the lemon grass or rind, ginger, lemon or other leaves and whole chillis and bring to the boil. Reduce the heat to low and simmer the mixture for 10 minutes. Remove from the heat, strain the stock and set it aside.

Pour the stock into a second saucepan and return to the boil. Stir in the fish sauce and lemon juice, then stir in the prawns (shrimp). Cook over moderate heat for 5 minutes, or until they are cooked through. Stir in the chopped chilli, spring onions (scallions) and coriander leaves and remove from the heat.

Transfer the mixture to a warmed tureen and serve at once.

Serves 6-8

Preparation and cooking time: 40 minutes

KAENG CHUD SAKU

(Tapioca Soup)   (Thailand)

Metric/Imperial	American
1.2l./2 pints chicken stock	5 cups chicken stock
225g./8oz. minced pork	8oz. ground pork
½ tsp. salt	½ tsp. salt
125g./4oz. tapioca	⅔ cup tapioca
225g./8oz. crabmeat, shell and cartilage removed	8oz. crabmeat, shell and cartilage removed
1 small Chinese cabbage, shredded	1 small Chinese cabbage, shredded
1 Tbs. soya sauce	1 Tbs. soy sauce

Bring the chicken stock to the boil in a large saucepan. Add the pork and salt, stirring constantly to separate the meat. Reduce the heat to low and stir in the tapioca. Simmer for 20 minutes, or until the pork is cooked.

Flake the crabmeat and stir into the soup with the cabbage. Cover and simmer for 2 to 4 minutes, or until the crabmeat is heated through.

Stir in the soy sauce before serving.

Serves 6-8

Preparation and cooking time: 35 minutes

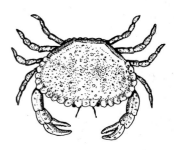

HINCHO

(Mixed Vegetable Soup)   (Burma)

The selection of vegetables given below is optional; any green vegetable, such as cauliflower, okra or cucumber could be added.

Metric/Imperial	American
1.2l./2 pints stock	5 cups stock
2 garlic cloves, crushed	2 garlic cloves, crushed
1 large onion, finely chopped	1 large onion, finely chopped
2 Tbs. dried prawns or 3 shelled fresh prawns	2 Tbs. dried shrimp or 3 shelled fresh shrimp
2 tsp. blachan (dried shrimp paste)	2 tsp. blachan (dried shrimp paste)
½ small Chinese cabbage, shredded	½ small Chinese cabbage, shredded
2 courgettes, thinly sliced	2 zucchini, thinly sliced
225g./8oz. pumpkin flesh, cubed	1⅓ cups cubed pumpkin flesh
pepper and salt	pepper and salt

Put the stock, garlic, onion, dried prawns or shrimp and blachan into a saucepan and bring to the boil. Add the remaining vegetables, adding those which take longest to cook first, and simmer until all are cooked through (about 5 minutes in all). Adjust seasoning and serve at once.

Serves 6-8

Preparation and cooking time: 20 minutes

MAH MI

(Singapore Soup Noodles)

Metric/Imperial	American
½kg./1lb. prawns, shelled and with the shells and heads reserved	1lb. shrimp, shelled and with the shells and heads reserved
salt and pepper	salt and pepper
3 Tbs. peanut oil	3 Tbs. peanut oil
3 garlic cloves, crushed	3 garlic cloves, crushed
4cm./1½in. piece of fresh root ginger, peeled and chopped	1½in. piece of fresh green ginger, peeled and chopped
225g./8oz. cooked pork, cut into strips	8oz. cooked pork, cut into strips
225g./8oz. bean sprouts	1 cup bean sprouts
125g./4oz. fine noodles or vermicelli	4oz. fine noodles or vermicelli
GARNISH	GARNISH
125g./4oz. tin crabmeat, shell and cartilage removed	4oz. can crabmeat, shell and cartilage removed
¼ cucumber, peeled and diced	¼ cucumber, peeled and diced
6 spring onions, chopped	6 scallions, chopped

First make the stock. Put the prawn or shrimp shells and heads into a saucepan and pour over about 1.2l./2 pints (5 cups) of water. Add salt and pepper to taste and bring to the boil. Reduce the heat to low and simmer the mixture for 30 minutes. Remove from the heat and strain the stock, reserving about 900ml./1½ pints (3½ cups). Set aside.

Heat the oil in a large saucepan. When it is very hot, add the garlic and ginger and stir-fry for 1 minute. Add the pork, prawns or shrimp and bean sprouts and stir-fry for 3 minutes. Pour over the reserved stock and bring to the boil. Stir in the noodles and cook the mixture for 5 minutes.

Transfer the mixture to a large serving bowl and garnish with the flaked crabmeat, cucumber and spring onions (scallions) before serving.
Serves 4-6
Preparation and cooking time: 1 hour

SOTO AYAM

(Chicken Soup)   (Indonesia)

Metric/Imperial	American
1 x 1½kg./3lb. chicken	1 x 3lb. chicken
1.75l./3 pints water	7½ cups water
salt and pepper	salt and pepper
2 medium onions, sliced	2 medium onions, sliced
3 Tbs. peanut oil	3 Tbs. peanut oil
2 garlic cloves, crushed	2 garlic cloves, crushed
4cm./1½in. piece of fresh root ginger, peeled and chopped	1½in. piece of fresh green ginger, peeled and chopped
2 red chillis, crumbled	2 red chillis, crumbled
1 tsp. blachan (dried shrimp paste)	1 tsp. blachan (dried shrimp paste)
1 tsp. turmeric	1 tsp. turmeric
2 tsp. ground coriander	2 tsp. ground coriander
½ tsp. grated nutmeg	½ tsp. grated nutmeg

GARNISH

125g./4oz. cooked vermicelli
4 Tbs. chopped spring onions
2 hard-boiled eggs, sliced
GARNISH

1 cup cooked vermicelli
4 Tbs. chopped scallions
2 hard-cooked eggs, sliced

Put the chicken into a large saucepan and pour over the water. Add salt and pepper to taste and one onion, and bring to the boil. Cover, reduce the heat to low and simmer the chicken for 1 hour, or until the chicken is cooked through. Remove from the heat. Transfer the chicken to a plate to cool and reserve the stock.

When the chicken is cool enough to handle, remove the skin and cut the meat into bite-sized pieces. Set aside.

Heat the oil in a large saucepan. When it is hot, add the remaining onion, the garlic, ginger, chillis and blachan and fry, stirring occasionally, until the onion is soft. Stir in the spices and fry for 1 minute. Pour over the stock and bring to the boil. Reduce the heat to low and simmer the soup for 15 minutes, skimming the surface occasionally.

Put the chicken meat and cooked vermicelli into a large tureen and pour over the stock. Add the spring onions (scallions) and egg slices before serving. Sometimes, dry fried chillis and sambal ulek are passed around in separate bowls to eat with the soup.
Serves 6-8
Preparation and cooking time: 1½ hours

MOHINGHA

(Fish Soup with Noodles)   (Burma)

Mohingha has often been described as the Burmese national dish – cooked and served on every conceivable occasion from family celebrations to roadside stalls. It is a meal in itself.

Metric/Imperial	American
½kg./1lb. whole fish, such as whiting, mackerel or herring	1lb. whole fish, such as whiting, mackerel or herring
600ml./1 pint water	2½ cups water
grated rind of 1 large lemon	grated rind of 1 large lemon
4 large onions, 2 finely chopped and 2 sliced	4 large onions, 2 finely chopped and 2 sliced
4 garlic cloves, crushed	4 garlic cloves, crushed
4cm./1½in. piece of fresh root ginger, peeled and chopped	1½in. piece of fresh green ginger, peeled and chopped
1 tsp. turmeric	1 tsp. turmeric
50ml./2fl.oz. sesame oil	¼ cup sesame oil
½ tsp. blachan (dried shrimp paste)	½ tsp. blachan (dried shrimp paste)
1 Tbs. fish sauce	1 Tbs. fish sauce
2 tsp. chick-pea flour	2 tsp. chick-pea flour
600ml./1 pint coconut milk	2½ cups coconut milk
¼ Chinese cabbage, shredded	¼ Chinese cabbage, shredded
350g./12oz. rice vermicelli	12oz. rice vermicelli
2 hard-boiled eggs, sliced	2 hard-cooked eggs, sliced
GARNISH	GARNISH
3 spring onions, chopped	3 scallions, chopped
2 Tbs. chopped coriander leaves	2 Tbs. chopped coriander leaves
1 lemon, cut into wedges	1 lemon, cut into wedges

Fillet the fish and put the heads, tails, skin and bones into a saucepan. Add the water and lemon rind and bring to the boil. Reduce the heat to low, cover the pan and simmer the stock for 15 minutes. Strain the liquid and set aside.

Meanwhile, put the chopped onions, garlic, ginger and turmeric into a blender and blend to a purée. Transfer to a small bowl. Heat the oil in a large saucepan. When it is hot, add the onion mixture and fry gently for 2 minutes, stirring constantly. Add the fish pieces and fry on both sides until they are lightly browned. Pour over the fish stock and bring to the boil.

Beat the blachan into the fish sauce, then stir in the flour. Stir the mixture into the mixture in the saucepan until it is thoroughly blended. Pour over the coconut milk and bring to the boil. Add the remaining onions and cabbage and reduce the heat to low. Cover the pan and simmer the soup for 15 minutes.

Meanwhile soak the rice vermicelli in warm water for 10 minutes or until it is cooked through. Drain and transfer to a warmed serving bowl.

Stir the egg slices into the fish soup, then transfer the mixture to a large, warmed tureen. Arrange the garnish ingredients in small, separate bowls.

To serve, spoon the vermicelli into individual serving bowls then pour over the fish soup. Garnish with spring onions (scallions), coriander leaves and lemon wedges to taste.

Serves 4
Preparation and cooking time : 2 hours

KAENG CHUD KAI HED

(Chicken and Mushroom Soup)   (Thailand)

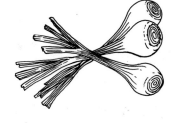

Metric/Imperial	American
1 x 2kg./4lb. chicken	1 x 4lb. chicken
1.2l./2 pints chicken stock	5 cups chicken stock
1 tsp. salt	1 tsp. salt
6 spring onions, finely chopped	6 scallions, finely chopped
2 Tbs. vegetable oil	2 Tbs. vegetable oil
2 garlic cloves, crushed	2 garlic cloves, crushed
2 Tbs. chopped coriander leaves	2 Tbs. chopped coriander leaves
125g./4oz. bean sprouts	½ cup bean sprouts
1 Tbs. fish sauce	1 Tbs. fish sauce
4 dried mushrooms, soaked in cold water for 30 minutes, drained and finely chopped	4 dried mushrooms, soaked in cold water for 30 minutes, drained and finely chopped
1 small cucumber, peeled (skin reserved) and flesh chopped	1 small cucumber, peeled (skin reserved) and flesh chopped

Put the chicken in a large saucepan and pour over the stock. Add the salt and spring onions (scallions), cover and bring to the boil. Reduce the heat to low and simmer for 1¼ hours, or until the chicken is cooked through. Remove from the heat. Transfer the chicken to a plate and reserve the stock.

When the chicken is cool enough to handle, tear it into shreds with your fingers. Set aside.

Heat the oil in a large saucepan. When it is hot, add the garlic, coriander and bean sprouts and stir-fry for 2 minutes. Add the chicken pieces, fish sauce and mushrooms and stir-fry for 3 minutes. Add the reserved stock and bring to the boil. Reduce the heat to low and simmer for 3 minutes.

Transfer to a warmed tureen and float curls of cucumber skin on the surface. Serve with the chopped cucumber flesh.

Serves 4-6
Preparation and cooking time : 2½ hours

(See over) Thailand is the home of Kaeng Chud Kai Hed, a filling chicken and mushroom soup.

NOODLES & RICE

RICE NOODLES WITH SPICY BEEF

(Thailand)

Metric/Imperial	American
½kg./1lb. rice noodles	1lb. rice noodles
3 Tbs. peanut oil	3 Tbs. peanut oil
1 onion, thinly sliced	1 onion, thinly sliced
4cm./1½in. piece of fresh root ginger, peeled and chopped	1½in. piece of fresh green ginger, peeled and chopped
1 green chilli, chopped	1 green chilli, chopped
700g./1½lb. rump steak, cut into strips	1½lb. rump steak, cut into strips
1 Tbs. fish sauce	1 Tbs. fish sauce
125g./4oz. roasted peanuts, crushed	1 cup roasted peanuts, crushed

Cook the noodles in boiling salted water for 5 minutes. Drain and pour over cold water. Drain again. Transfer to a warmed serving dish and keep hot.

Heat the oil in a large frying-pan. When the oil is hot, add the onion, ginger, chilli and beef and stir-fry for 5 minutes. Add the fish sauce and remove the pan from the heat.

Spoon the mixture over the noodles and sprinkle over the peanuts before serving.

Serves 4-6
Preparation and cooking time: 15 minutes

PANCIT

(Fried Noodles) (Philippines)

Pancit in Filipino means simply noodles – usually egg – which are served in a whole variety of delicious ways. The recipe given below is a fairly basic version and can be added to or subtracted from at will – for instance, cooked pork or fish fillets can be blended in pancit, and bean sprouts could be substituted for the cabbage suggested here.

MetricI/mperial	American
450g./1lb. egg noodles	1lb. egg noodles
½kg./1lb. shrimps, in the shell	1lb. shrimp, in the shell
300ml./10fl.oz. water	1¼ cups water
50g./2oz. lard	4 Tbs. lard
1 large onion, chopped	1 large onion, chopped
2 garlic cloves, crushed	2 garlic cloves, crushed
1 cooked chicken breast, skinned, boned and cut into strips	1 cooked chicken breast, skinned, boned and cut into strips
225g./8oz. cooked ham, cut into strips	8oz. cooked ham, cut into strips
5 leaves Chinese cabbage, shredded	5 leaves Chinese cabbage, shredded
¼ cucumber, chopped or sliced	¼ cucumber, chopped or sliced
2 Tbs. soya sauce	2 Tbs. soy sauce

Salt and pepper
3 spring onions, chopped

Salt and pepper
3 scallions, chopped

Cook the egg noodles in boiling, salted water for 5 minutes, or until they are just tender. Drain under cold running water and set aside.

Put the shrimps and water into a large saucepan and bring to the boil. Reduce the heat to low and simmer for 10 minutes. Remove from the heat and strain and reserve about 250ml./8fl.oz. (1 cup) of the cooking liquid. Shell and devein the shrimps and set them aside.

Melt half the lard in a large, deep frying-pan. Add the noodles and stir-fry for 3 minutes, or until they are evenly browned (cook them in batches if necessary). Using tongs or a slotted spoon, transfer the noodles to a plate and keep warm while you cook the meat and vegetables.

Melt the remaining lard in the frying-pan. Add the onion and garlic and fry, stirring occasionally, until the onion is soft. Add the chicken, ham, cabbage and cucumber and stir-fry for 3 minutes. Stir in the shrimps, the reserved cooking liquid, soy sauce and salt and pepper to taste. Bring the liquid to the boil. Return the noodles to the pan and stir-fry for a further 2 minutes, or until they are heated through.

Transfer the mixture to a warmed serving bowl and garnish with the spring onions (scallions) before serving.
Serves 6
Preparation and cooking time: 50 minutes

RICE NOODLES WITH PORK & PRAWNS OR SHRIMPS

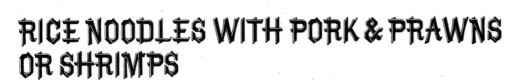

(Thailand)

Metric/Imperial	American
½kg./1lb. rice noodles	1lb. rice noodles
4 Tbs. peanut oil	4 Tbs. peanut oil
350g./12oz. pork fillet, cut into strips	12oz. pork tenderloin, cut into strips
225g./8oz. prawns, shelled	8oz. shrimp, shelled
6 spring onions, chopped	6 scallions, chopped
1 garlic clove, crushed	1 garlic clove, crushed
6 dried mushrooms, soaked in cold water for 30 minutes, drained and sliced	6 dried mushrooms, soaked in cold water for 30 minutes, drained and sliced
½ tsp. sugar	½ tsp. sugar
2 Tbs. fish sauce	2 Tbs. fish sauce
1 Tbs. chopped coriander leaves	1 Tbs. chopped coriander leaves

Cook the noodles in boiling salted water for 5 minutes. Drain and pour over cold water. Drain again. Transfer to a warmed serving dish and keep hot.

Heat the oil in a large frying-pan. When it is hot, add the pork strips and stir-fry for 3 minutes. Add the prawns or shrimp and stir-fry for 3 minutes. Add the spring onions (scallions), garlic and mushrooms and stir-fry for 2 minutes. Stir in the remaining ingredients and remove the pan from the heat.

Spoon the mixture over the noodles and garnish with coriander leaves before serving.
Serves 4-6
Preparation and cooking time: 20 minutes

(See over) Rice noodles form the basis of many Oriental dishes and none is more delicious than this Thai version, Rice Noodles with Pork and Prawns or Shrimps.

21

BAHMI GORENG

(Indonesian Fried Noodles)   (Indonesia)

Metric/Imperial	American
225g./8oz. fine egg noodles (vermicelli)	8oz. fine egg noodles (vermicelli)
4 Tbs. peanut oil	4 Tbs. peanut oil
1 onion, finely chopped	1 onion, finely chopped
2 garlic cloves, crushed	2 garlic cloves, crushed
2½cm./1in. piece of fresh root ginger, peeled and finely chopped	1in. piece of fresh green ginger, peeled and finely chopped
½ tsp. blachan (dried shrimp paste)	½ tsp. blachan (dried shrimp paste)
1 tsp. dried chillis or sambal ulek	1 tsp. dried chillis or sambal ulek
1 chicken breast, boned and cut into thin strips	1 chicken breast, skinned, boned and cut into thin strips
50g./2oz. frozen prawns, thawed	¼ cup frozen shrimp, thawed
1 large celery stalk, sliced	1 large celery stalk, sliced
2 Chinese or white cabbage leaves, shredded	2 Chinese or white cabbage leaves, shredded
2 Tbs. soya sauce	2 Tbs. soy sauce
GARNISH	GARNISH
1 Tbs. chopped peanuts	1 Tbs. chopped peanuts
2 spring onions, chopped	2 scallions, chopped

Cook the noodles in boiling salted water for 3 to 5 minutes, or until they are just tender. Drain and rinse under cold running water, then set aside.

Heat the oil in a large deep frying-pan. When it is hot, add the onion, garlic, ginger, blachan and sambal ulek and stir-fry for 3 minutes. Stir in the chicken and prawns (shrimp) and cook for a further 2 minutes. Add the celery and cabbage and stir-fry for 2 minutes. Stir in the noodles and cook for a further 2 to 3 minutes, or until they are heated through. Stir in the soy sauce.

Transfer the mixture to a large, warmed serving bowl and garnish with the chopped peanuts and spring onions (scallions) before serving.
Serves 3-4
Preparation and cooking time: 30 minutes

MIKROB

(Fried Crisp Noodles)   (Thailand)

Metric/Imperial	American
vegetable oil for deep frying	vegetable oil for deep frying
½kg./1lb. rice vermicelli	1lb. rice vermicelli
50ml./2fl.oz. peanut oil	¼ cup peanut oil
4 spring onions, chopped	4 scallions, chopped
3 garlic cloves, crushed	3 garlic cloves, crushed
175g./6oz. pork fillet, cut into strips	6oz. pork tenderloin, cut into strips
1 chicken breast, skinned, boned and cut into strips	1 chicken breast, skinned, boned and cut into strips
125g./4oz. shelled prawns, chopped	4oz. shelled shrimp, chopped
1 bean curd cake, chopped	1 bean curd cake, chopped
225g./8oz. bean sprouts	1 cup bean sprouts
2 Tbs. sugar	2 Tbs. sugar
4 Tbs. vinegar	4 Tbs. vinegar

4 Tbs. fish sauce	4 Tbs. fish sauce
1 Tbs. lemon juice	1 Tbs. lemon juice
1 Tbs. grated orange rind	1 Tbs. grated orange rind
5 eggs, lightly beaten	5 eggs, lightly beaten
GARNISH	GARNISH
chopped coriander leaves	chopped coriander leaves
1 dried red chilli, crumbled	1 dried red chilli, crumbled

Fill a large deep-frying pan one-third full with the oil and heat it until it is hot. Carefully lower the vermicelli (straight from the packet, in batches), into the hot oil and fry until it is golden brown. Using a slotted spoon, remove from the oil and drain on kitchen towels. Keep hot while you cook the remaining vermicelli in the same way.

Heat the peanut oil in a deep frying-pan. When it is very hot, add the spring onions (scallions) and garlic and fry, stirring occasionally, until the spring onions (scallions) are soft. Add the meat, prawns (shrimp), bean curd and bean sprouts and stir-fry for 5 minutes. Add the sugar, vinegar, fish sauce, lemon juice and orange rind and mix well. Stir in the eggs and cook, stirring occasionally, until they have set.

Arrange the vermicelli in a warmed serving bowl. Pour over the meat mixture and garnish with the coriander leaves and chilli before serving.

Serves 6-8
Preparation and cooking time: 45 minutes

PHAT WUN SEN

(Fried Vermicelli)   (Thailand)

Metric/Imperial	American
350g./12oz. rice vermicelli	12oz. rice vermicelli
50ml./2fl.oz. peanut oil	¼ cup peanut oil
2 garlic cloves, crushed	2 garlic cloves, crushed
1 red chilli, chopped	1 red chilli, chopped
4 spring onions, chopped	4 scallions, chopped
1 pork chop, boned and cut into strips	1 pork chop, boned and cut into strips
125g./4oz. frozen prawns, thawed	4oz. frozen shrimp, thawed
8 dried mushrooms, soaked in cold water for 30 minutes, drained and sliced	8 dried mushrooms, soaked in cold water for 30 minutes, drained and sliced
2 carrots, thinly sliced	2 carrots, thinly sliced
1½ Tbs. fish sauce	1½ Tbs. fish sauce
1 Tbs. malt vinegar	1 Tbs. cider vinegar
1½ tsp. sugar	1½ tsp. sugar
salt and pepper	salt and pepper
2 Tbs. chopped coriander leaves	2 Tbs. chopped coriander leaves

Put the rice vermicelli into a large bowl and just cover with boiling water. Set aside to soak for 10 minutes, then drain thoroughly and set aside.

Meanwhile, heat the oil in a large saucepan. When it is hot, add the garlic, chilli and spring onions (scallions) and stir-fry for 2 minutes. Add the pork and stir-fry for a further 2 minutes. Add the prawns (shrimp), mushrooms and carrots and stir-fry for 1 minute. Add the fish sauce, vinegar, sugar and salt and pepper to taste and bring to the boil. Stir in the vermicelli and continue to stir-fry for a further 2 minutes, or until the mixture is throughly blended and the vermicelli heated through.

Transfer the mixture to a warmed serving dish and garnish with the coriander leaves before serving.
Serves 4-6
Preparation and cooking time: 1 hour

FRIED RICE

(Malaysia)

Metric/Imperial	American
350g./12oz. long-grain rice, soaked in cold water for 30 minutes and drained	2 cups long-grain rice, soaked in cold water for 30 minutes and drained
2 tsp. salt	2 tsp. salt
650ml./22fl.oz. water	2¾ cups water
50ml./2fl.oz. vegetable oil	¼ cup vegetable oil
2 medium onions, chopped	2 medium onions, chopped
2 red chillis, chopped	2 red chillis, chopped
½ tsp. blachan (dried shrimp paste)	½ tsp. blachan (dried shrimp paste)
1 garlic clove, crushed	1 garlic clove, crushed
2 tsp. ground coriander	2 tsp. ground coriander
175g./6oz. cooked shrimps, shelled	6oz. cooked shrimp, shelled
175g./6oz. cooked lamb or beef, sliced	6oz. cooked lamb or beef, sliced
2 tsp. soft brown sugar mixed with 1 Tbs. treacle and 2 Tbs. soya sauce	2 tsp. soft brown sugar, mixed with 1 Tbs. molasses and 2 Tbs. soy sauce
GARNISH	GARNISH
1 Tbs. butter	1 Tbs butter
2 eggs, lightly beaten	2 eggs, lightly beaten
¼ tsp. salt	¼ tsp. salt
2 Tbs. vegetable oil	2 Tbs. vegetable oil
2 red chillis, sliced	2 red chillis, sliced
2 onions, thinly sliced	2 onions, thinly sliced
½ cucumber, peeled and diced	½ cucumber, peeled and diced
6 spring onions, sliced	6 scallions, sliced

Put the rice, 1 teaspoon of salt and the water into a saucepan and bring to the boil. Reduce the heat to low, cover the pan and simmer for 15 to 20 minutes, or until the rice is tender and the water is absorbed.

Heat the oil in a large saucepan. When it is hot, add the onions and fry, stirring occasionally, until they are golden brown. Add the chillis, blachan, garlic and coriander and fry for 5 minutes, stirring constantly.

Stir in the shrimps and meat and fry for 1 to 2 minutes, or until they are well mixed with the spices. Stir in the rice, the soy sauce mixture and remaining salt. Reduce the heat to low and cook for 10 minutes, stirring occasionally.

Meanwhile, prepare the garnishes. Melt the butter in a small frying-pan. Add the eggs and salt and cook until the bottom is set and lightly browned. Turn the omelet over and fry for another 2 minutes. Remove from the heat and slide the omelet on to a plate. Cut into strips and set aside.

Wipe out the pan and heat the oil in it over moderately high heat. When it is hot, add the chillis and fry for 2 minutes, stirring constantly. Add the onions and fry, stirring occasionally, until they are golden brown. Remove from the heat and set aside.

When the rice mixture is ready, turn it out on to a warmed serving platter. Scatter the cucumber, spring onions (scallions), fried onions, chillis and the shredded omelet on top. Serve at once.
Serves 6
Preparation and cooking time: 1½ hours

NASI GORENG

(Indonesian Rice)   (Indonesia)

Metric/Imperial	American
350g./12oz. long-grain rice, soaked in cold water for 30 minutes and drained	2 cups long-grain rice, soaked in cold water for 30 minutes and drained
725ml./1¼ pints water	3 cups water
1 tsp. salt	1 tsp. salt
2 Tbs. vegetable oil	2 Tbs. vegetable oil
3 eggs, lightly beaten	3 eggs, lightly beaten
1 medium onion, finely chopped	1 medium onion, finely chopped
2 green chillis, finely chopped	2 green chillis, finely chopped
1 garlic clove, crushed	1 garlic clove, crushed
½kg./1lb. cooked chicken meat, cut into thin slices	1lb. cooked chicken meat, cut into thin slices
225g./8oz. prawns, shelled and chopped	8oz. shrimp, shelled and chopped
2 celery stalks, finely chopped	2 celery stalks, finely chopped
2 Tbs. soya sauce	2 Tbs. soy sauce

Put the rice into a large saucepan. Pour over the water and salt and bring to the boil. Reduce the heat to low, cover and simmer for 15 to 20 minutes, or until the rice is tender and the liquid absorbed. Set aside.

Heat half the oil in a small frying-pan. When it is hot, add the eggs and fry for 3 minutes on each side, or until they form an omelet. Slide the omelet on to a plate and cut into thin strips. Set aside.

Heat the remaining oil in a large frying-pan. When the oil is hot, add the onion, chillis and garlic and fry, stirring occasionally, until the onion is soft. Add the chicken, prawns or shrimp and celery and cook, stirring occasionally, until they are well mixed. Stir in the cooked rice, soy sauce and the omelet strips and cook for 3 to 5 minutes, or until all the ingredients are warmed through and well blended.

Transfer the mixture to a warmed serving bowl and serve at once.
Serves 6-7
Preparation and cooking time: 45 minutes

KAO PAD

(Thai Fried Rice)   (Thailand)

Metric/Imperial	American
4 Tbs. peanut oil	4 Tbs. peanut oil
1 large onion, chopped	1 large onion, chopped
1 red chilli, chopped	1 red chilli, chopped
225g./8oz. pork fillet, cut into strips	8oz. pork tenderloin, cut into strips
225g./8oz. frozen prawns	8oz. frozen shrimp
125g./4oz. crabmeat, shell and cartilage removed	4oz. crabmeat, shell and cartilage removed
3 eggs, lightly beaten	3 eggs, lightly beaten
2 Tbs. fish sauce	2 Tbs. fish sauce
350g./12oz. cooked long-grain rice	4 cups cooked long-grain rice
3 Tbs. tomato purée	3 Tbs. tomato paste
6 spring onions, chopped	6 scallions, chopped
2 Tbs. chopped coriander leaves	2 Tbs. chopped coriander leaves

Heat the oil in a large saucepan. When it is hot, add the onion and chilli and fry, stirring occasionally, until the onion is soft. Add the pork strips and stir-fry for 3 minutes. Add the prawns (shrimp) and crabmeat to the mixture and stir-fry for 2 minutes.

Break the eggs into the centre of the mixture and quickly stir until they are thoroughly combined. Stir in the fish sauce, cooked rice and tomato purèe (paste) and stir-fry for 5 minutes or until the rice is completely heated through and the mixture is blended.

Transfer the mixture to a large warmed serving bowl and garnish with the spring onions (scallions) and chopped coriander leaves.

Serve at once.

Serves 4-6

Preparation and cooking time: 50 minutes

Indonesian Liver and Rice is a satisfying one-dish meal, adapted from the traditional Indonesian Nasi Goreng.

INDONESIAN LIVER & RICE

Metric/Imperial	American
450g./1lb. long-grain rice, soaked in cold water for 30 minutes and drained	2⅔ cups long-grain rice, soaked in cold water for 30 minutes and drained
1.2l./2 pints water	5 cups water
1 tsp. salt	1 tsp. salt
3 Tbs. peanut oil	3 Tbs. peanut oil
3 eggs, lightly beaten	3 eggs, lightly beaten
4 spring onions, chopped	4 scallions, chopped
75g./3oz. mushrooms, sliced	¾ cup sliced mushrooms
1 tinned pimiento, drained and finely chopped	1 canned pimiento, drained and finely chopped
1 red chilli, chopped	1 red chilli, chopped
2 garlic cloves, crushed	2 garlic cloves, crushed
5cm./2in. piece of fresh root ginger, peeled and finely chopped	2in. piece of fresh green ginger, peeled and finely chopped
2 Tbs. soya sauce	2 Tbs. soy sauce
LIVER	LIVER
4 Tbs. soya sauce	4 Tbs. soy sauce
4 Tbs. beef stock	4 Tbs. beef stock
1 Tbs. wine vinegar	1 Tbs. wine vinegar
2 Tbs. water	2 Tbs. water
salt and pepper	salt and pepper
1 garlic clove, crushed	1 garlic clove, crushed
10cm./4in. piece of fresh root ginger, peeled and chopped	4in. piece of fresh green ginger, peeled and chopped
2 tsp. cornflour	2 tsp. cornstarch
1½kg./3lb. lambs liver, thinly sliced	3lb. lambs liver, thinly sliced
50ml./2fl.oz. peanut oil	¼ cup peanut oil
2 celery stalks, chopped	2 celery stalks, chopped
350g./12oz. bean sprouts	1½ cups bean sprouts

First prepare the liver. Combine the soy sauce, stock, vinegar, water, seasoning, garlic, half the ginger and cornflour (cornstarch) in a shallow bowl. Add the liver slices and set aside to marinate for 45 minutes, basting frequently.

Meanwhile, prepare the rice. Put the rice, water and salt into a large saucepan and bring to the boil. Cover, reduce the heat to low and simmer for 15 to 20 minutes, or until the rice is tender and the liquid absorbed. Remove from the heat and set aside.

Heat 1 tablespoon of the oil in a small frying-pan. When it is hot, add the eggs and fry on each side until they are set in a thin omelet. Slide the omelet on to a plate and cut into thin strips. Set aside.

Preheat the oven to very cool 130°C (Gas Mark ½, 250°F).

Heat the remaining oil in a large frying-pan. When it is hot, add the spring onions (scallions), mushrooms, pimiento, chilli, garlic and ginger and fry until the spring onions (scallions) are soft. Stir in the rice, soy sauce and omelet strips and fry for 3 minutes, stirring occasionally. Transfer to an ovenproof dish and keep hot in the oven while you cook the liver.

Heat the oil in a large frying-pan. When it is hot, add the remaining ginger and fry for 2 minutes. Increase the heat to moderately high and add the liver and marinade to the pan. Fry, stirring and turning occasionally, for 6 minutes. Stir in the remaining ingredients and fry for 3 minutes, or until the liver slices are cooked through.

Remove the dish from the oven and arrange the liver slices over the rice. Spoon over the sauce and vegetables and serve at once.

Serves 8
Preparation and cooking time: 1 hour

YELLOW RICE

(Indonesia)

Metric/Imperial	American
3 Tbs. vegetable oil	3 Tbs. vegetable oil
1 large onion, finely chopped	1 large onion, finely chopped
2 garlic cloves, crushed	2 garlic cloves, crushed
1 Tbs. turmeric	1 Tbs. turmeric
salt and pepper	salt and pepper
1 tsp. finely chopped lemon grass or grated lemon rind	1 tsp. finely chopped lemon grass or grated lemon rind
450g./1lb. long-grain rice, soaked in cold water for 30 minutes and drained	$2\frac{2}{3}$ cups long-grain rice, soaked in cold water for 30 minutes and drained
600ml./1 pint water	$2\frac{1}{2}$ cups water
300ml./10fl.oz. coconut milk	$1\frac{1}{4}$ cups coconut milk
2 bay leaves	2 bay leaves
GARNISH	GARNISH
3 hard-boiled eggs, quartered	3 hard-cooked eggs, quartered
125g./4oz. roasted peanuts	$\frac{2}{3}$ cup roasted peanuts
2 bananas, sliced	2 bananas, sliced
coriander sprigs	coriander sprigs

Heat the oil in a large saucepan. When it is hot, add the onion and garlic and fry, stirring occasionally, until the onion is soft. Stir in the turmeric, seasoning to taste, lemon grass or rind and rice and fry for 3 minutes, stirring constantly. Pour over the water and coconut milk and bring to the boil. Reduce the heat to low, add the bay leaves and cover the pan. Simmer for 15 to 20 minutes, or until the rice is tender and the liquid absorbed. Discard the bay leaves.

Transfer the rice to a warmed serving dish, shaping it into a dome. Garnish with the eggs, peanuts, bananas and coriander and serve at once.

Serves 6
Preparation and cooking time: 35 minutes

INDONESIAN SPICED RICE

Metric/Imperial	American
50g./2oz. tamarind	$\frac{1}{4}$ cup tamarind
250ml./8fl.oz. boiling water	1 cup boiling water
350g./12oz. long-grain rice, soaked in cold water for 30 minutes and drained	2 cups long-grain rice, soaked in cold water for 30 minutes and drained
1 tsp. salt	1 tsp. salt
2 Tbs. dark treacle	2 Tbs. molasses
1 tsp. ground cumin	1 tsp. ground cumin
1 Tbs. soya sauce	1 Tbs. soy sauce
1 Tbs. ground coriander	1 Tbs. ground coriander
1 tsp. hot chilli powder	1 tsp. hot chilli powder
$\frac{1}{2}$ medium coconut, grated	$\frac{1}{2}$ medium coconut, grated
4 Tbs. vegetable oil	4 Tbs. vegetable oil
1 medium onion, thinly sliced	1 medium onion, thinly sliced
125g./4oz. chopped peanuts	$\frac{2}{3}$ cup chopped peanuts
450ml./15fl.oz. boiling chicken stock	2 cups boiling chicken stock

Put the tamarind pulp into a bowl and pour over the water. Set aside to cool. Pour the contents of the bowl through a strainer into a saucepan, pressing as much pulp through as possible.

Half fill a large saucepan with water and bring to the boil. Add the rice and salt and boil briskly for 2 minutes. Drain, discard the cooking liquid and set the rice aside.

Stir the treacle (molasses), cumin, soy sauce, coriander and chilli powder into the tamarind liquid. Bring to the boil, then cook for 5 to 10 minutes, stirring occasionally, or until the mixture thickens slightly. Stir in the rice and grated coconut, remove from the heat and keep hot.

Heat the oil in a large saucepan. When it is hot, add the onion and fry, stirring occasionally, for 3 minutes. Add the peanuts and fry for 5 minutes, or until both they and the onions are browned. Stir in the rice mixture and cook for a further 2 minutes. Pour over the stock, cover and reduce the heat to low. Simmer for 10 to 15 minutes, or until the rice is tender and the liquid absorbed.

Transfer to a warmed serving bowl and serve at once.

Serves 4-6
Preparation and cooking time: 1¼ hours

FRIED RICE WITH MEATS

In Vietnam, the rice for this dish is traditionally 'roasted' in an earthenware pot. However, the method suggested below is somewhat easier for less experienced rice cooks to follow and produces authentic – and excellent – results.

Metric/Imperial	American
75ml./3fl. oz. peanut oil	6 Tbs. peanut oil
350g./12oz. long- or medium-grain rice soaked in cold water for 30 minutes and drained	2 cups long- or medium-grain rice, soaked in cold water for 30 minutes and drained
600ml./1 pint boiling water	2½ cups boiling water
4cm./1½in. piece of fresh root ginger, peeled and chopped	1½in. piece of fresh green ginger, peeled and chopped
1 garlic clove, crushed	1 garlic clove, crushed
4 spring onions, chopped	4 scallions, chopped
1 chicken breast, skinned, boned and cut into thin strips	1 chicken breast, skinned, boned and cut into thin strips
125g./4oz. lean pork meat, cut into thin strips	4 oz. lean pork meat, cut into thin strips
8 dried mushrooms, soaked in cold water for 30 minutes, drained and chopped	8 dried mushrooms, soaked in cold water for 30 minutes, drained and chopped
1 Tbs. fish sauce	1 Tbs. fish sauce
2 eggs	2 eggs
1 Tbs. chopped coriander leaves	1 Tbs. chopped coriander leaves

Heat half the oil in a large saucepan. When it is hot, add the rice and stir-fry for 2 minutes, or until it becomes opaque. Reduce the heat to very low and simmer the rice gently for a further 10 minutes, stirring occasionally. Pour over the water and return to the boil. Reduce the heat to low, cover the pan and simmer the rice for 10 to 15 minutes, or until it is tender and the liquid absorbed.

Meanwhile, heat the remaining oil in a large, deep frying-pan. When it is hot, add the ginger, garlic and about three-quarters of the spring onions (scallions) and stir-fry for 2 minutes. Add the chicken and pork meat and continue to stir-fry for 4 minutes, or until the meat is cooked through. Add the mushrooms and fish sauce and stir-fry for 2 minutes. Remove the pan from the heat.

When all the liquid has been absorbed from the rice, make a well in the centre and carefully pour in the chicken and pork mixture. Break the eggs into the centre of the chicken and pork mixture and stir-fry briskly into the meat, then the rice until the eggs are 'cooked'.

Transfer the mixture to a warmed serving bowl or platter and garnish with the remaining spring onion (scallion) and chopped coriander leaves before serving.
Serves 4
Preparation and cooking time: 1 hour 10 minutes

NASI KUNING LENGKAP

(Festive Rice) (Indonesia)

Metric/Imperial	American
2 Tbs. peanut oil	2 Tbs. peanut oil
1 large onion, chopped	1 large onion, chopped
2 garlic cloves, crushed	2 garlic cloves, crushed
1 tsp. chopped lemon grass or grated lemon rind	1 tsp. chopped lemon grass or grated lemon rind
1 tsp. turmeric	1 tsp. turmeric
$\frac{1}{2}$ tsp. laos powder	$\frac{1}{2}$ tsp. laos powder
3 curry or bay leaves	3 curry or bay leaves
1 tsp. salt	1 tsp. salt
450g./1lb. long-grain rice, soaked in cold water for 30 minutes and drained	$2\frac{2}{3}$ cups long-grain rice, soaked in cold water for 30 minutes and drained
1.2l./2 pints coconut milk	5 cups coconut milk
GARNISH	GARNISH
1 Tbs. vegetable oil	1 Tbs. vegetable oil
2 small eggs, beaten	2 small eggs, beaten
4 spring onions, chopped	4 scallions, chopped
2 red chillis, quartered	2 red chillis, quartered
2 green chillis, quartered	2 green chillis, quartered
2 hard-boiled eggs, sliced	2 hard-cooked eggs, sliced
$\frac{1}{3}$ cucumber, sliced or cut into 2$\frac{1}{2}$cm./ 1in. lengths	$\frac{1}{3}$ cucumber, sliced or cut into 1in. lengths

Heat the peanut oil in a large saucepan. When it is hot, add the onion and garlic and fry, stirring occasionally, until the onion is soft. Stir in the lemon grass or rind, turmeric, laos powder, curry or bay leaves and salt. Add the rice and stir-fry for 2 to 3 minutes, or until it becomes opaque. Pour over the coconut milk and bring to the boil. Reduce the heat to low, cover the pan and simmer the mixture for 20 to 25 minutes, or until the rice is cooked and tender and the liquid absorbed.

Meanwhile, make the garnish. Heat the vegetable oil in a small frying-pan. When it is hot, add the eggs and cook until the bottom is set and lightly browned. Turn the omelet over and cook for another 2 minutes. Remove from the heat and slide the omelet onto a plate. Cut into strips and set aside.

When the rice is cooked, transfer to a large serving dish. Using greaseproof or waxed paper, carefully pat the rice into a conical shape (if you have a cone-shaped strainer, you can put the rice into this, then carefully unmould it on to the dish). Put the chillis in rows up and down the shaped rice and scatter the omelet strips over the top. Arrange the hard-boiled (hard-cooked) egg slices and cucumbers (plus any of the other garnishes suggested) around the base of the rice.
Serve at once.
Serves 6
Preparation and cooking time: 1$\frac{1}{4}$ hours

BEEF

STIR-FRIED BEEF

(Malaysia)

Metric/Imperial	American
3 Tbs. dark soya sauce	3 Tbs. dark soy sauce
2 garlic cloves, crushed	2 garlic cloves, crushed
2 tsp. cornflour	2 tsp. cornstarch
1 tsp. sugar	1 tsp. sugar
700g./1½lb. rump steak, cut into strips	1½lb. rump steak, cut into strips
4 Tbs. vegetable oil	4 Tbs. vegetable oil
7½cm./3in. piece of fresh root ginger, peeled and chopped	3in. piece of fresh green ginger, peeled and chopped
225g./8oz. bean sprouts	1 cup bean sprouts

Combine the soy sauce, garlic, cornflour (cornstarch) and sugar in a shallow bowl. Add the beef strips and mix well. Cover and set aside for 30 minutes, stirring occasionally.

Heat the oil in a large frying-pan. When it is hot, add the ginger and stir-fry for 3 minutes. Add the beef mixture and stir-fry for 5 minutes. Stir in the bean sprouts and stir-fry for a further 4 minutes.

Spoon into a warmed bowl and serve at once.

Serves 4-6
Preparation and cooking time: 50 minutes

MORCON

(Beef Roll with Tomato Sauce)   (Philippines)

Metric/Imperial	American
1½kg./3lb. beef skirt, cut crosswise into 2 or 3 pieces and flattened by beating to ½cm./¼in. thick	3lb. beef flank, cut crosswise into 2 or 3 pieces and flattened by beating to ¼in. thick
½ tsp. salt	½ tsp. salt
¼ tsp. pepper	¼ tsp. pepper
1 Tbs. lemon juice	1 Tbs. lemon juice
1 garlic clove, crushed	1 garlic clove, crushed
4 cooked ham slices	4 cooked ham slices
4 hard-boiled eggs, sliced	4 hard-cooked eggs, sliced
125g./4oz. Cheddar cheese, thinly sliced	4oz. Cheddar cheese, thinly sliced
225g./8oz. green olives, stoned and chopped	2 cups green olives, pitted and chopped
75ml./3fl.oz. vegetable oil	⅓ cup vegetable oil
25g./1oz. butter	2 Tbs. butter
½kg./1lb. tomatoes, blanched, peeled and chopped	1lb. tomatoes, blanched, peeled and chopped
1 Tbs. soya sauce	1 Tbs. soy sauce
125ml./4fl.oz. water	½ cup water
25g./1oz. beurre manié	2 Tbs. beurre manié

Put the beef pieces on a flat surface, overlapping to make a large oblong. Pound the overlapping edges together to seal. Sprinkle over the salt, pepper, lemon juice and garlic.

Arrange the ham slices over the beef, then the egg slices, in lines. Top with the cheese. Sprinkle over the olives and a third of the oil. Roll up Swiss (jelly) roll fashion and secure with string at intervals to keep the shape.

Melt the butter with the remaining oil in a large saucepan. Add the meat roll and brown, turning from time to time, for 10 minutes. Reduce the heat to low and add the tomatoes, soy sauce and water and bring to the boil. Cover and simmer for 45 minutes to 1 hour, or until the meat is cooked through.

Remove the roll to a carving board and discard the string. Cut into 2½cm./1in. slices and arrange on a heated serving dish. Keep warm.

Bring the pan juices to the boil and add the beurre manié, stirring constantly until it has dissolved. Cook for 3 to 5 minutes, or until the sauce has thickened. Pour over the meat before serving.

Serves 6
Preparation and cooking time: 1¾ hours

Top: Morcon (beef roll with tomato sauce), is a popular Filipino dish, where the Spanish influence is clearly discernible. Below: Malaysia is the home of Rendang, a spicy beef stew which is adapted from an Indian curry. If you prefer your curries to be less than lethal, you can adjust the amount of chilli powder used in a recipe, or seed fresh chillis – the heat is in the seeds rather than the pods.

RENDANG

(Spicy Beef)   (Malaysia)

Metric/Imperial	American
1kg./2lb. topside of beef, cut into cubes	2lb. top round of beef, cut into cubes
2 garlic cloves, crushed	2 garlic cloves, crushed
2½cm./1in. piece of fresh root ginger, peeled and chopped	1in. piece of fresh green ginger, peeled and chopped
1 green chilli, chopped	1 green chilli, chopped
1 tsp. salt	1 tsp. salt
2 tsp. hot chilli powder	2 tsp. hot chilli powder
1 Tbs. ground coriander	1 Tbs. ground coriander
1 tsp. ground cumin	1 tsp. ground cumin
1 tsp. turmeric	1 tsp. turmeric
1 tsp. sugar	1 tsp. sugar
2 medium onions, chopped	2 medium onions, chopped
1 stalk lemon grass or 1 x 5cm./2in. piece finely pared lemon rind	1 stalk lemon grass or 1 x 2in. piece of finely pared lemon rind
juice of ½ lemon	juice of ½ lemon
600ml./1 pint thick coconut milk	2½ cups thick coconut milk

Put the beef cubes in a large bowl. Mix the garlic, ginger, chilli and salt together and rub the mixture into the cubes. Set aside for 30 minutes.

Combine the chilli powder, coriander, cumin, turmeric, sugar, onions, lemon grass or rind, lemon juice and coconut milk in a saucepan and bring to the boil. Add the beef cubes and bring to the boil again, stirring constantly. Reduce the heat to moderately low and cook uncovered, for 1 to 1¼ hours, or until the beef is cooked through and tender. Reduce the heat to low and cook, stirring constantly, until the meat is golden brown and all the liquid has evaporated.

Remove from the heat and transfer the meat to a warmed serving dish. Serve at once.

Serves 4-6
Preparation and cooking time: 2¼ hours.
Note: great care must be taken during the last stage of cooking. The heat must be carefully adjusted and the ingredients stirred constantly or else the meat will burn and the dish will be ruined.

Bun Bo could be described as the Vietnamese national dish – a platter of vermicelli, one of succulent meat garnished with crushed peanuts, and a third containing refreshing salad. And, of course, always on the Vietnamese table is Nuoc Cham, a dipping sauce made from fish sauce. It is used as a condiment in much the same way as ketchup is used in the West.

BUN BO

(Stir-fried Beef with Noodles)   (Vietnam)

Metric/Imperial	American
½kg./1lb. rice vermicelli	1lb. rice vermicelli
50ml./2fl.oz. peanut oil	¼ cup peanut oil
1kg./2lb. rump steak, cut into strips	2lb. rump steak, cut into strips
2 onions, chopped	2 onions, chopped
1 Tbs. fish sauce	1 Tbs. fish sauce
125g./4oz. roasted peanuts, crushed	⅔ cup roasted peanuts, crushed
GARNISH	GARNISH
1 small crisp lettuce, shredded	1 small crisp lettuce, shredded
½ small cucumber, chopped	½ small cucumber, chopped
3 spring onions (green part only), chopped	3 scallions (green part only), chopped
1 serving nuoc cham (page 92)	1 serving nuoc cham (page 92)

Cook the vermicelli in boiling salted water for 5 minutes. Drain, refresh under cold water, then keep hot while you cook the meat.

Heat the oil in a large frying-pan. When it is hot, add the meat and onions and stir-fry for 5 minutes. Stir in the fish sauce and stir-fry for a further 1 minute.

To serve, assemble the salad ingredients on one platter, the vermicelli on another and the meat on a third. Sprinkle the meat mixture with the crushed peanuts and serve the dish with the fish sauce.

Serves 6-8
Preparation and cooking time: 35 minutes

JAVANESE CURRY

Metric/Imperial	American
1 tsp. cumin seeds	1 tsp. cumin seeds
1 Tbs. coriander seeds	1 Tbs. coriander seeds
2 Tbs. blanched almonds	2 Tbs. blanched almonds
2 onions, coarsely chopped	2 onions, coarsely chopped
3 red or green chillis	3 red or green chillis
4cm./1½in. piece of fresh root ginger, peeled	1½in. piece of fresh green ginger, peeled
3 garlic cloves	3 garlic cloves
½ tsp. blachan (dried shrimp paste)	½ tsp. blachan (dried shrimp paste)
50ml./2fl.oz. vegetable oil	¼ cup vegetable oil
1kg./2lb. stewing steak, cubed	2lb. chuck steak, cubed
300ml./10fl.oz. water	1¼ cups water
1 tsp. salt	1 tsp. salt
½ tsp. laos powder (optional)	½ tsp. laos powder (optional)
1 tsp. chopped lemon grass or grated lemon rind	1 tsp. chopped lemon grass or grated lemon rind
25g./1oz. tamarind	2 Tbs. tamarind
125ml./4fl.oz. boiling water	½ cup boiling water
225g./8oz. green cabbage, shredded	8oz. green cabbage, shredded
8 spring onions, cut into lengths	8 scallions, cut into lengths
175ml./6fl.oz. thick coconut milk	¾ cup thick coconut milk

Put the cumin, coriander and almonds in a blender with the onions, chillis, ginger,

garlic and blachan. Blend to a paste, adding enough water to prevent the blades from sticking.

Heat the oil in a large saucepan. When it is hot, add the spice paste and fry for 5 minutes, or until it comes away from the sides of the pan. Add the beef cubes and fry until they are evenly browned. Pour in the water and stir in the salt, laos, and lemon grass and bring to the boil. Reduce the heat to low, cover and simmer for 2 to 2½ hours, or until the beef is cooked through and tender.

Meanwhile, put the tamarind into a bowl and pour over the water. Set aside until it is cool. Pour the contents of the bowl through a strainer into a bowl, pressing as much of the pulp through as possible.

Add the shredded cabbage, spring onions (scallions), coconut milk and tamarind liquid to the curry and bring to the boil again. Stir and allow to boil for 2 minutes.

Remove from the heat and transfer to a warmed serving dish. Serve at once.
Serves 4-6
Preparation and cooking time: 2½ hours

Javanese Curry is hot and very spicy. Serve with cooling raitas and sambals and plain rice for the best effect.

38

BEEF SATE

(Indonesia)

Metric/Imperial	American
1 Tbs. coriander seeds	1 Tbs. coriander seeds
2 garlic cloves	2 garlic cloves
2 green chillis	2 green chillis
1 tsp. turmeric	1 tsp. turmeric
2½cm./1in. piece of fresh root ginger, peeled	1in. piece of fresh green ginger, peeled
2 medium onions, chopped	2 medium onions, chopped
2 Tbs. lemon juice	2 Tbs. lemon juice
1 Tbs. soya sauce	1 Tbs. soy sauce
4 Tbs. peanut oil	4 Tbs. peanut oil
700g./1½lb. rump steak, cubed	1½lb. rump steak, cubed
250ml./8fl.oz. thick coconut milk	1 cup thick coconut milk
125ml./4fl.oz. water	½ cup water
1 curry or bay leaf	1 curry or bay leaf

Put the coriander, garlic, chillis, turmeric, ginger, onions, lemon juice and soy sauce into a blender and blend to a smooth purée. Alternatively, pound the ingredients in a mortar with a pestle until they are smooth.

Heat the oil in a large saucepan. When it is hot, add the spice paste and fry for 5 minutes, stirring constantly. Add the meat cubes, and remaining ingredients and bring to the boil. Reduce the heat to low and simmer for 40 to 45 minutes, or until the meat is cooked through and the sauce is very thick. Set aside until the meat is cool enough to handle, then transfer the meat to a plate. Remove the curry or bay leaf and keep the sauce warm.

Preheat the grill (broiler) to high. Thread the cubes on to skewers and arrange on the rack of the grill (broiler). Grill (broil) the meat for 5 minutes on each side, or until it is golden brown, basting frequently with the sauce.

Pile the skewers on to a warmed serving platter and serve with the remaining sauce.

Serves 6
Preparation and cooking time: 1¼ hours

SATE MANIS

(Sweet Sate)   (Indonesia)

Metric/Imperial	American
1½ Tbs. jaggery or soft brown sugar	1½ Tbs. jaggery or soft brown sugar
3 Tbs. soya sauce	3 Tbs. soy sauce
3 Tbs. water	3 Tbs. water
2 tsp. lemon juice	2 tsp. lemon juice
2 garlic cloves, crushed	2 garlic cloves, crushed
2 red or green chillis, seeded and chopped	2 red or green chillis, seeded and chopped
salt and pepper	salt and pepper
700g./1½lb. rump steak, cut into 2½cm./1in. cubes	1½lb. rump steak, cut into 1in. cubes
1 Tbs. peanut oil	1 Tbs. peanut oil

SAUCE	SAUCE
1 Tbs. peanut oil	1 Tbs. peanut oil
2 garlic cloves, crushed	2 garlic cloves, crushed
1½ tsp. dried chillis or sambal ulek	1½ tsp. dried chillis or sambal ulek
1 tsp. blachan (dried shrimp paste)	1 tsp. blachan (dried shrimp paste)
¼ tsp. laos powder (optional)	¼ tsp. laos powder (optional)
½ tsp. jaggery or soft brown sugar	½ tsp. jaggery or soft brown sugar
5 Tbs. peanut butter	5 Tbs. peanut butter
350ml./12fl. oz. coconut milk or water	1½ cups coconut milk or water
2 Tbs. lemon juice	2 Tbs. lemon juice

Put the jaggery or brown sugar, soy sauce, water and lemon juice into a large shallow dish. Stir in the garlic and chilli and add salt and pepper to taste. Arrange the beef cubes in the mixture and baste well. Set aside at room temperature for 4 hours, basting occasionally. Remove the cubes from the marinade mixture and pat dry with kitchen towels. Discard the marinade.

Preheat the grill (broiler) to moderately high. Thread the beef cubes on to skewers and arrange the skewers on the rack of the grill (broiler) and grill (broil) for 15 to 20 minutes, turning and basting occasionally with the tablespoon of peanut oil, or until the beef is cooked through and tender.

Meanwhile, to make the sauce, heat the oil in a frying-pan. When it is hot, add the garlic and sambal ulek and stir-fry for 1 minute. Stir in the blachan, laos powder and jaggery or brown sugar, until the sugar has dissolved. Add the peanut butter and stir until it becomes smooth. Gradually add the coconut milk or water, stirring constantly and bring to the boil. Remove the pan from the heat. (The sauce should be of a thick pouring consistency so thin down if necessary with more coconut milk or water).

To serve, arrange the beef, on skewers, across a serving dish and spoon a little of the sauce on top. Pour the remaining sauce into a warmed sauceboat and serve it with the sate.

Serves 4-6
Preparation and cooking time: 4½ hours

REMPAH

(Beef and Coconut Patties)   (Indonesia)

Rempah are a sort of Eastern hamburger and are just as delicious to eat and as easy to make as their Western equivalent! They are usually eaten as a snack or hors d'oeuvre and the servings below reflect this. However, they would make an excellent main dish served with a rice or noodle dish and some vegetables – but in this case make double quantities to serve 6-8.

Metric/Imperial	American
125g./4oz. desiccated coconut	1 cup shredded coconut
225g./8oz. minced beef	8oz. ground beef
1 garlic clove, crushed	1 garlic clove, crushed
¼ tsp. blachan (dried shrimp paste) (optional)	¼ tsp. blachan (dried shrimp paste) (optional)
1 tsp. ground coriander	1 tsp. ground coriander
½ tsp. ground cumin	½ tsp. ground cumin
¼ tsp. laos powder or ground ginger	¼ tsp. laos powder or ground ginger
1 egg, lightly beaten	1 egg, lightly beaten
50g./2oz. cornflour	½ cup cornstarch
125ml./4fl.oz. peanut oil	½ cup peanut oil

Put the coconut into a bowl and moisten with about 4 tablespoons of boiling water. Then stir in all the remaining ingredients, except the cornflour (cornstarch) and oil and beat until they are smooth and well blended.

Using your hands, shape the mixture into about 12 small patty shapes. Dip each shape into the cornflour (cornstarch), shaking off any excess.

Heat about half the oil in a large frying-pan. When it is very hot, add half the patties and fry for about 5 minutes on each side, or until they are cooked through and golden. Remove from the heat and drain on kitchen towels. Keep the rempah hot while you cook the remaining batch of patties in the same way.

Serves 6-8
Preparation and cooking time: 40 minutes

KAENG MASAMAN

(Mussulman Curry)   (Thailand)

Metric/Imperial	American
1kg./2lb. braising steak, cubed	2lb. chuck steak, cubed
900ml./1½ pints thick coconut milk	3¾ cups thick coconut milk
125g./4oz. roasted peanuts	⅔ cup roasted peanuts
1 Tbs. fish sauce (optional)	1 Tbs. fish sauce (optional)
25g./1oz. tamarind	2 Tbs. tamarind
50ml./2fl.oz. boiling water	¼ cup boiling water
2 Tbs. lime or lemon juice	2 Tbs. lime or lemon juice
2 tsp. soft brown sugar	2 tsp. soft brown sugar
CURRY PASTE	CURRY PASTE
1 Tbs. hot chilli powder	1 Tbs. hot chilli powder
2 Tbs. ground coriander	2 Tbs. ground coriander
2 tsp. ground cumin	2 tsp. ground cumin
½ tsp. ground fennel	½ tsp. ground fennel
1 tsp. laos powder	1 tsp. laos powder
1 tsp. ground ginger	1 tsp. ground ginger
½ tsp. ground cardamom	½ tsp. ground cardamom
½ tsp. ground cinnamon	½ tsp. ground cinnamon
½ tsp. ground cloves	½ tsp. ground cloves
2 tsp. chopped lemon grass or grated lemon rind	2 tsp. chopped lemon grass or grated lemon rind
3 Tbs. peanut oil	3 Tbs. peanut oil
4 garlic cloves, crushed	4 garlic cloves, crushed
1 large onion, chopped	1 large onion, chopped
½ tsp. blachan (dried shrimp paste)	½ tsp. blachan (dried shrimp paste)

To make the curry paste, combine the chilli powder, coriander, cumin, fennel, laos, ginger, cardamom, cinnamon and cloves. Stir in the lemon grass or rind. Heat the oil in a small frying-pan. When it is hot, add the garlic, onion and blachan and fry, stirring occasionally, until the onion is soft. Remove from the heat and set aside to cool. When the mixture has cooled a little, put it into a blender and blend to a purée. Stir the purée into the ground spice mixture until all the ingredients are well blended.

Put the beef and coconut milk into a saucepan and bring to the boil. Add the peanuts and fish sauce and reduce the heat to low. Simmer the mixture, uncovered, for 2 hours, or until the beef is cooked through and tender. Using a slotted spoon, transfer the meat to a plate.

Set the pan with the cooking liquid over high heat and bring to the boil. Continue to boil rapidly until the gravy has reduced by about one-third.

Meanwhile, put the tamarind into a bowl and pour over the water. Set aside until it is cool. Pour the contents of the bowl through a strainer into a bowl, pressing as much of the pulp through as possible. Set aside.

Stir the curry paste into the pan containing the gravy, then return the beef cubes to the pan. Simmer for 5 minutes, basting the beef thoroughly in the liquid. Stir in the tamarind water, lime or lemon juice and brown sugar and heat until just below boiling.

Serve at once.

Serves 4-6

Preparation and cooking time: $2\frac{1}{2}$ hours

SEMUR BANKA

(Beef in Soy Sauce)   (Indonesia)

Metric/Imperial	American
25g./1oz. tamarind	2 Tbs. tamarind
125ml./4fl.oz. boiling water	$\frac{1}{2}$ cup boiling water
50ml/2fl.oz. groundnut oil	$\frac{1}{4}$ cup groundnut oil
2 medium onions, thinly sliced	2 medium onions, thinly sliced
3 garlic cloves, crushed	3 garlic cloves, crushed
4cm./1½in. piece of fresh root ginger, peeled and finely chopped	1½in. piece of fresh green ginger, peeled and finely chopped
3 cloves, crushed	3 cloves, crushed
¼ tsp. grated nutmeg or garam masala	¼ tsp. grated nutmeg or garam masala
¼ tsp. black pepper	¼ tsp. black pepper
1kg./2lb. stewing or braising steak, cut into 4cm./1½in. pieces	2lb. chuck steak, cut into 1½in. pieces
1 tsp. salt	1 tsp. salt
2 tsp. soft brown sugar mixed with 1 Tbs. treacle and 2 Tbs. dark soy sauce	2 tsp. soft brown sugar mixed with 1 Tbs. molasses and 2 Tbs. dark soy sauce
150ml./5fl.oz. water	$\frac{2}{3}$ cup water

Put the tamarind into a bowl and pour over the water. Set aside until it is cool. Pour the contents of the bowl through a strainer into a bowl, pressing as much of the pulp through as possible. Set aside the liquid.

Heat the oil in a large deep frying-pan. When it is hot, add the onions and fry, stirring occasionally, until they are soft. Add the garlic, ginger, spices and pepper and fry for 3 minutes, stirring frequently. Add the meat and increase the heat to moderately high. Cook the meat, turning from time to time, until it is deeply and evenly browned.

Stir in the remaining ingredients, including the reserved tamarind, and bring to the boil. Reduce the heat to low, cover the pan and simmer for 2 to $2\frac{1}{2}$ hours, or until the meat is cooked through and tender and the sauce is thick and rather rich in texture.

Remove from the heat, transfer the mixture to a large, warmed serving platter and serve at once.

Serves 6

Preparation and cooking time: 3 hours

CURRY PUFFS

(Malaysia)

Metric/Imperial	American
350g./12oz. puff pastry	2 cups puff pastry
FILLING	FILLING
2 Tbs. vegetable oil	2 Tbs. vegetable oil
1 onion, finely chopped	1 onion, finely chopped
1cm./½in. piece of fresh root ginger, peeled and chopped	2in. piece of fresh green ginger, peeled and chopped
1 garlic clove, crushed	1 garlic clove, crushed
2 red or green chillis, finely chopped	2 red or green chillis, finely chopped
1 tsp. hot chilli powder	1 tsp. hot chilli powder
½ tsp. turmeric	½ tsp. turmeric
½ tsp. ground coriander	½ tsp. ground coriander
½ tsp. salt	½ tsp. salt
225g./8oz. minced beef	8oz. ground beef
1 tomato, blanched, peeled and chopped	1 tomato, blanched, peeled and chopped
3 Tbs. frozen cooked peas	3 Tbs. frozen cooked peas
2 Tbs. lime or lemon juice	2 Tbs. lime or lemon juice

Heat the oil in a frying-pan. When it is hot, add the onion, ginger, garlic and chillis and fry, stirring occasionally, until the onion is soft. Stir in the spices and salt and fry for 3 minutes, stirring constantly. Add the beef and fry for 5 minutes, or until it loses its pinkness. Add the remaining filling ingredients and cook for 5 minutes. Set aside. Preheat the oven to fairly hot 190°C (Gas Mark 5, 375°F).

Roll the dough out to a circle about ¼cm./⅛in. thick. Using a 10cm./4in. pastry cutter, cut it into circles.

Place about 2 teaspoonfuls of the filling mixture slightly to the side of each circle and dampen the edges with water. Fold over one-half of the circle to make a semi-circle and press the edges to seal.

Put the semi-circles on a baking sheet and bake for 30 to 35 minutes, or until they are golden brown. Serve warm.

Makes 20 puffs
Preparation and cooking time: 1 hour

BO XAO MANG

(Beef with Bamboo Shoot)   (Vietnam)

Metric/Imperial	American
50ml./2fl.oz. peanut oil	¼ cup peanut oil
½kg./1lb. rump steak, cut into thin strips	1lb. rump steak, cut into thin strips
400g./14oz. tin bamboo shoot, drained and cut into strips about the same size as the meat	14oz. can bamboo shoot, drained and cut into strips about the same size as the meat
4 spring onions, chopped	4 scallions, chopped
1 garlic clove, crushed	1 garlic clove, crushed
1 Tbs. fish sauce	1 Tbs. fish sauce
salt and pepper	salt and pepper
2 Tbs. roasted sesame seeds, crushed	2 Tbs. roasted sesame seeds, crushed

Two Malaysian dishes: Top: Curry Puffs, succulent semi-circles of pastry enclosing a spicy meat filling; and Below: Stir-Fried Beef, a Malay-Chinese dish starring rump steak and bean sprouts.

Heat half the oil in a large, deep frying-pan. When it is very hot, add the beef strips and stir-fry for 2 minutes, or until they just lose their pinkness. Using a slotted spoon, transfer them to a plate and keep warm.

Add the remaining oil to the frying-pan. When it is hot, add the bamboo shoot, spring onions (scallions) and garlic to the pan and stir-fry for 3 minutes. Add the fish sauce and salt and pepper to taste, stirring until they are well blended.

Return the beef to the pan and stir in the sesame seeds. Continue to stir-fry for a further 1 minute, or until they are heated through.

Transfer the mixture to a warmed serving dish and serve at once.

Serves 4
Preparation and cooking time: 30 minutes

RENDANG DAGING

(Fried Beef Curry)   (Indonesia)

Metric/Imperial	American
1 large onion, chopped	1 large onion, chopped
3 garlic cloves, crushed	3 garlic cloves, crushed
4cm./1½in. piece of fresh root ginger, peeled and chopped	1½in. piece of fresh green ginger, peeled and chopped
450ml./15fl. oz. thick coconut milk	2 cups thick coconut milk
1½ tsp. hot chilli powder	1½ tsp. hot chilli powder
1 tsp. turmeric	1 tsp. turmeric
2 tsp. ground coriander	2 tsp. ground coriander
1 tsp. ground cumin	1 tsp. ground cumin
½ tsp. laos powder	½ tsp. laos powder
50ml./2fl. oz. vegetable oil	¼ cup vegetable oil
1kg./2lb. braising steak, cut into strips or small cubes	2lb. chuck steak, cut into strips or small cubes
2 Tbs. desiccated coconut, roasted	2 Tbs. shredded coconut, roasted
½ tsp. chopped lemon grass or grated lemon rind	½ tsp. chopped lemon grass or grated lemon rind
25g./1oz. tamarind	2 Tbs. tamarind
125ml./4fl. oz. boiling water	½ cup boiling water
1 tsp. soft brown sugar	1 tsp. soft brown sugar

Put the onion, garlic and ginger into a blender with about 50ml./2fl.oz. (¼ cup) of coconut milk and blend to a smooth, thick paste. Stir in the ground chilli powder, turmeric, coriander, cumin and laos powder until the mixture is thoroughly blended. Set aside.

Heat the oil in a large saucepan. When it is hot, add the beef pieces and fry, stirring occasionally, until they are browned. Add the coconut mixture and fry for 3 minutes, stirring constantly. Add a spoonful or two of water if the mixture becomes too dry. Stir in the desiccated (shredded) coconut and lemon grass or rind then pour over the remaining coconut milk. Bring to the boil. Reduce the heat to low, cover the pan and simmer the mixture for 1½ hours, stirring occasionally.

Meanwhile, put the tamarind into a bowl and pour over the boiling water. Set aside until it is cool. Put the contents of the bowl through a strainer into the saucepan, pressing as much of the pulp through as possible.

Stir the tamarind liquid and brown sugar into the meat mixture until it is well blended. Re-cover and continue to simmer for a further 30 minutes, or until the meat is cooked through and tender.

Transfer the mixture to a warmed serving bowl and serve at once.

Serves 4-6
Preparation and cooking time: 2¾ hours

LAMB

SAMBAI GORENG ATI

(Spiced Liver)   (Indonesia)

The best type of liver to use in this recipe is probably calf's liver but lamb's liver or chicken livers could be substituted with very little loss of taste. Don't use pig or ox liver, however; they are rather tough and require longer, slower cooking.

Metric/Imperial	American
1 onion, chopped	1 onion, chopped
1 garlic clove, crushed	1 garlic clove, crushed
2 tsp. chopped dried chillis or sambal ulek	2 tsp. chopped dried chillis or sambal ulek
½ tsp. blachan (dried shrimp paste)	½ tsp. blachan (dried shrimp paste)
1 tsp. laos powder	1 tsp. laos powder
1 tsp. chopped lemon grass or grated lemon rind	1 tsp. chopped lemon grass or grated lemon rind
3 Tbs. peanut oil	3 Tbs. peanut oil
½kg./1lb. liver, cut into strips	1lb. liver, cut into strips
2 tsp. soft brown sugar	2 tsp. soft brown sugar
175ml./6fl.oz. thick coconut milk	¾ cup thick coconut milk

Put the onion, garlic, chillis or sambal ulek and blachan into a blender and blend to a smooth purée. Stir the laos powder and lemon grass or rind into the mixture.

Heat the oil in a large frying-pan. When it is hot, add the spice mixture and stir-fry for 3 minutes. Add the liver strips and stir-fry for 3 minutes, or until they lose their pinkness. Stir in the sugar and coconut milk and bring to the boil. Reduce the heat to low and simmer the mixture for 5 minutes, or until the liver is cooked through and tender and the liquid has thickened slightly.

Transfer the mixture to a warmed serving dish and serve at once.
Serves 4
Preparation and cooking time: 30 minutes

GULEH KAMBLING

(Lamb Curry)   (Indonesia)

Metric/Imperial	American
5cm./2in. piece of fresh root ginger, peeled and chopped	2in. piece of fresh green ginger, peeled and chopped
2 garlic cloves, crushed	2 garlic cloves, crushed
5 green chillis, chopped	5 green chillis, chopped
1 tsp. ground lemon grass or finely grated lemon rind	1 tsp. ground lemon grass or finely grated lemon rind
½ tsp. laos powder	½ tsp. laos powder
2 tsp. turmeric	2 tsp. turmeric
2 tsp. salt	2 tsp. salt
50g./2oz. ground almonds	⅓ cup ground almonds

7 Tbs. vegetable oil	7 Tbs. vegetable oil
2 medium onions, chopped	2 medium onions, chopped
1¼kg./2½lb. boned leg of lamb, cubed	2½lb. boned leg of lamb, cubed
225g./8oz. tomatoes, blanched, peeled and chopped	8oz. tomatoes, blanched, peeled and chopped
300ml./10fl.oz. coconut milk	1¼ cups coconut milk
1 small onion, sliced	1 small onion, sliced
6 cloves, lightly crushed	6 cloves, lightly crushed
1 Tbs. crushed coriander seeds	1 Tbs. crushed coriander seeds
1 tsp. crushed cumin seeds	1 tsp. crushed cumin seeds

Another delicious lamb curry from Indonesia, Guleh Kambling is also sometimes served as part of a rijsttafel. However, it also makes an excellent Western-style meal served with rice, salad and chutneys.

Combine the ginger, garlic, chillis, lemon grass or rind, laos, turmeric, salt and ground almonds with 1 tablespoon of oil and 1 tablespoon of water to make a paste. Add more water if necessary. Set aside.

Heat 50ml./2fl.oz. (¼ cup) of the oil in a large saucepan. When it is hot, add the chopped onions and fry, stirring occasionally, until they are golden brown. Add the spice paste and fry for 5 minutes, stirring frequently. Add the lamb cubes and fry for 15 to 20 minutes, or until they have completely lost their pinkness and are thoroughly coated with the spice mixture.

Stir in the tomatoes and cook for 1 minute. Add the milk and bring to the boil. Reduce the heat to low, cover and simmer the curry for 1 hour, or until the meat is cooked through and tender and the gravy is thick.

Meanwhile, heat the remaining oil in a small frying-pan. When it is hot, add the sliced onion and spices and fry, stirring frequently, until the onion is golden brown. Ten minutes before the end of the cooking time, stir the onion and spice mixture into the lamb.

Transfer the mixture to a warmed serving dish and serve at once.
Serves 8
Preparation and cooking time: 2 hours

MURTABA

(Savoury Lamb Crêpes)   (Singapore)

Metric/Imperial	American
350g./12oz. wholewheat flour	3 cups wholewheat flour
½ tsp. salt	½ tsp. salt
250ml./8fl.oz. lukewarm water	1 cup lukewarm water
50g./2oz. ghee or clarified butter	4 Tbs. ghee or clarified butter
FILLING	FILLING
3 Tbs. vegetable oil	3 Tbs. vegetable oil
1 onion, finely chopped	1 onion, finely chopped
1 garlic clove, crushed	1 garlic clove, crushed
2 green chillis, chopped	2 green chillis, chopped
350g./12oz. minced lamb	12oz. ground lamb
1 tomato, blanched, peeled and chopped	1 tomato, blanched, peeled and chopped
3 Tbs. cooked green peas	3 Tbs. cooked green peas
salt and pepper	salt and pepper
1 tsp. garam masala	1 tsp. garam masala
1 egg, beaten	1 egg, beaten

First make the dough. Put the flour and salt into a bowl and make a well in the centre. Pour in the water and beat briskly until a stiff dough is formed. Cover the bowl and set the dough aside for 1 hour.

Meanwhile, make the filling. Heat the oil in a medium frying-pan. When it is hot, add the onion, garlic and chillis and fry until the onion is soft, stirring occasionally. Stir in the lamb and continue to fry the mixture until the meat loses its pinkness. Stir in the tomato, peas and salt and pepper to taste and cook for a further 3 minutes. Reduce the heat to low and simmer the mixture for 10 minutes. Sprinkle over the garam masala, remove from the heat and keep warm.

Remove the dough from the bowl and knead the dough gently. On a slightly oiled board, divide the mixture into balls, then gently press each ball out into a very thin crêpe (as thin as possible without tearing the dough – it should resemble strudel pastry).

Melt a little ghee in a frying-pan or griddle and gently ease in one of the crêpes. Carefully brush a little beaten egg over the exposed side of the crêpe and spoon over some filling. Fold over the sides of the crêpe so that the filling is completely enclosed and fry for 1 minute. Carefully turn over the crêpe and cook for a further 1 minute, then remove from the pan. Cook the other crêpes in the same way, then serve hot.

Serves 6-8 (as a snack or hors d'oeuvre)
Preparation and cooking time: 1¾ hours

LAMB SATE

(Indonesia)

Metric/Imperial	American
3 garlic cloves, crushed	3 garlic cloves, crushed
4 Tbs. soya sauce	4 Tbs. soy sauce
1 Tbs. soft brown sugar	1 Tbs. soft brown sugar
1 small onion, grated	1 small onion, grated
1 Tbs. lemon juice	1 Tbs. lemon juice
½ tsp. salt	½ tsp. salt
1kg./2lb./boned lean lamb, cubed	2lb. boned lean lamb, cubed
SAUCE	SAUCE
150ml./5fl.oz. soya sauce	⅔ cup soy sauce
1 tsp. ground coriander	1 tsp. ground coriander
1 garlic clove, crushed	1 garlic clove, crushed
1 green or red chilli, crumbled	1 green or red chilli, crumbled
3 Tbs. soft brown sugar	3 Tbs. soft brown sugar
2 Tbs. dark treacle	2 Tbs. molasses
1 Tbs. lemon juice	1 Tbs. lemon juice

Sates come in all shapes and forms in Indonesia and can be made from almost any ingredient. While Lamb Sate is more unusual than pork, chicken or beef, it is equally delicious. And in this case the accompanying sauce has a soy sauce base instead of peanuts. Sates are perfect for summer barbecues.

Mix the garlic, soy sauce, sugar, onion, lemon juice and salt in a small bowl. Add the meat cubes and set aside to marinate for 1 hour, basting occasionally.

Meanwhile, combine all the sauce ingredients in a medium saucepan. Set over moderate heat and bring to the boil, stirring constantly. Reduce the heat to low and simmer for 5 minutes. Remove from the heat and keep warm while you cook the sate.

Preheat the grill (broiler) to high. Thread the cubes on to skewers and arrange on the rack of the grill (broiler). Grill (broil) for 8 minutes, turn and grill (broil) for a further 6 minutes or until the meat is cooked through.

Pile the skewers on to a warmed serving platter. Pour the sauce into a small bowl and serve at once, with the kebabs.

Serves 8
Preparation and cooking time: 1½ hours

PORK

THIT KHO

(Pork Stew)   (Vietnam)

This is a northern Vietnamese dish, often served during the New Year festival. Belly or bacon of pork is probably the cut the Vietnamese would use but if you prefer leaner meat use blade or even leg.

Metric/Imperial	American
3 Tbs. peanut oil	3 Tbs. peanut oil
2 Tbs. sugar	2 Tbs. sugar
1kg./2lb. pork meat (with fat), cut into cubes	2lb. pork meat (with fat), cut into cubes
3 Tbs. fish sauce	3 Tbs. fish sauce
1 Tbs. soya sauce	1 Tbs. soy sauce
6 spring onions, chopped	6 scallions, chopped
3 hard-boiled eggs	3 hard-cooked eggs

Heat the oil in a large saucepan. When it is hot, stir in the sugar and cook until it browns slightly. Add the pork cubes and cook, basting with the sugar mixture, until they are browned. Add the fish sauce and soy sauce, and stir-fry for 1 minute. Pour over enough cold water just to cover and bring to the boil. Reduce the heat to low and simmer, uncovered, for 2 to 2½ hours, or until the liquid has reduced by about half, and the meat is very tender.

   Add the spring onions (scallions) and sliced eggs and simmer for 5 minutes before serving.
Serves 6
Preparation and cooking time: 2¼ hours

VIETNAMESE PORK LOAF

Metric/Imperial	American
½kg./1lb. minced pork	1lb. ground pork
8 dried mushrooms, soaked in cold water for 30 minutes, drained, stalks removed and chopped	8 dried mushrooms, soaked in cold water for 30 minutes, drained, stalks removed and chopped
4 spring onions, chopped	4 scallions, chopped
3 eggs, beaten	3 eggs, beaten
2 tsp. fish sauce	2 tsp. fish sauce
salt and black pepper	salt and black pepper

Put all the ingredients into a bowl and mix well. Arrange the mixture in a small, greased loaf pan and cover with a double thickness of foil. Place in the top of a steamer or in a large pan one-third full of boiling water. Steam for 1 hour.

   Remove the pan from the heat and unwrap the loaf. Leave the loaf in the pan for 10 minutes, then transfer to a chopping board. Cut into thin slices and serve with salad.
Serves 4
Preparation and cooking time: 1½ hours

MAH HO

(Galloping Horses)   (Thailand)

This exotically named dish is a typically Thai mixture of the sweet and savoury – savoury minced (ground) pork served on slices or rounds of sweet fruit. Pineapple is the fruit suggested here but more exotic oriental fruit such as rambutans could also be used. Mah ho is usually served as an hors d'oeuvre.

Metric/Imperial	American
2 Tbs. peanut oil	2 Tbs. peanut oil
1 garlic clove, crushed	1 garlic clove, crushed
1 small onion, finely chopped	1 small onion, finely chopped
350g./12oz. minced pork	12oz. ground pork
3 Tbs. roasted peanuts, ground	3 Tbs. roasted peanuts, ground
3 Tbs. jaggery or brown sugar	3 Tbs. jaggery or brown sugar
salt and pepper	salt and pepper
1 fresh pineapple, peeled, cored and cut into rounds	1 fresh pineapple, peeled, cored and cut into rounds
1 dried red chilli, crumbled	1 dried red chilli, crumbled
2 Tbs. chopped coriander leaves	2 Tbs. chopped coriander leaves

Heat the oil in a large frying-pan. When it is hot, add the garlic and onion and fry, stirring occasionally, until the onion is soft. Stir in the minced (ground) pork and fry until it loses its pinkness. Add the roasted peanuts, jaggery or sugar and seasoning to taste. Reduce the heat to low and simmer the mixture for 10 to 15 minutes, or until the pork is cooked through and the mixture is thick and dryish. Remove from the heat.

Arrange the pineapple rounds on a large serving platter. Carefully spoon the mixture over the rounds, doming it up slightly in the middle. Garnish with crumbled red chilli and the coriander leaves. Serve at once.
Serves 8-10
Preparation and cooking time: 35 minutes

PO CHERO

(Mixed Meat and Chick-Pea Ragout)   (Philippines)

Metric/Imperial	American
4 chicken pieces, cut into large bite-sized pieces	4 chicken pieces, cut into large bite-sized pieces
½kg./1lb. pork fillet, cut into large cubes	1lb. pork tenderloin, cut into large cubes
3 hot sausages, halved	3 hot sausages, halved
2 medium onions, sliced	2 medium onions, sliced
salt and pepper	salt and pepper
50ml./2fl.oz. vegetable oil	¼ cup vegetable oil
3 spring onions, chopped	3 scallions, chopped
3 garlic cloves, crushed	3 garlic cloves, crushed
2 sweet potatoes, cubed	2 sweet potatoes, cubed
½ white cabbage, shredded	½ white cabbage, shredded
400g./14oz. tin chick-peas, drained	14oz. can chick-peas, drained
1 Tbs. sugar	1 Tbs. sugar
2 Tbs. tomato purée	2 Tbs. tomato paste

Put the chicken pieces, pork, sausages, onions and salt and pepper to taste in a large saucepan. Just cover with water and bring to the boil. Cover the pan, reduce the heat to low and simmer for 50 minutes to 1¼ hours, or until the meat is cooked through. Remove from the heat, transfer the meat to a plate and strain and reserve 300ml./10fl.oz. (1¼ cups) of the cooking liquid.

Heat the oil in a large, deep frying-pan. When it is hot, add the spring onions (scallions) and garlic and fry for 3 minutes. Pour over the strained liquid and bring to the boil. Add the sweet potato cubes, reduce the heat to low and simmer for 30 minutes. Stir in the meat pieces, cabbage, chick-peas, sugar and tomato purée (paste), and bring to the boil. Reduce the heat to low, cover and simmer for 10 minutes, or until the cabbage is just cooked through and all the meats are tender.

Adjust the seasoning and serve at once.

Serves 8
Preparation and cooking time: 2¼ hours

SWEET & SOUR SPARERIBS

(Singapore)

Metric/Imperial	American
1½kg./3lb. American-style spareribs, cut into 2in. pieces	3lb. spareribs, cut into 2-rib serving pieces
2 garlic cloves, crushed	2 garlic cloves, crushed
3 Tbs. peanut oil	3 Tbs. peanut oil
5cm./2in. piece of fresh root ginger, peeled and chopped	2in. piece of fresh green ginger, peeled and chopped
1 large green pepper, pith and seeds removed and sliced	1 large green pepper, pith and seeds removed and sliced
1 large red pepper, pith and seeds removed and sliced	1 large red pepper, pith and seeds removed and sliced
175g./6oz. tin pineapple chunks, juice reserved	6oz. can pineapple chunks, juice reserved
1½ Tbs. wine vinegar	1½ Tbs. wine vinegar
1½ Tbs. soya sauce	1½ Tbs. soy sauce
1 Tbs. soft brown sugar	1 Tbs. soft brown sugar
1 Tbs. cornflour, mixed to a paste with 2 Tbs. water	1 Tbs. cornstarch, mixed to a paste with 2 Tbs. water

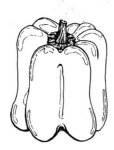

Preheat the oven to hot 220°C (Gas Mark 7, 425°F). Rub the spareribs with half the garlic and arrange them in a roasting pan. Roast for 30 minutes.

Meanwhile, heat the oil in a large frying-pan. When it is hot, add the remaining garlic and ginger and cook for 1 minute. Add the peppers and fry for 5 minutes, stirring occasionally. Stir in the pineapple chunks and fry for 3 minutes. Add the reserved pineapple juice, vinegar, soy sauce and sugar and bring to the boil.

Reduce the oven temperature to moderate 180°C (Gas Mark 4, 350°F).

Remove the ribs from the oven and pour off the fat. Stir in the pineapple mixture, basting the ribs thoroughly, and return the pan to the oven. Cook for 1 hour, basting occasionally, or until the ribs are golden brown and crisp. Remove from the oven and transfer the ribs to a serving plate.

Put the roasting pan over low heat and stir in the cornflour (cornstarch) mixture. Bring to the boil, stirring constantly, then cook until the sauce has thickened slightly and become translucent.

Pour the sauce over the ribs and serve at once.

Serves 6-8
Preparation and cooking time: 1¾ hours

PORK ADOBO

(The Philippines)

Metric/Imperial	American
1½kg./3lb. pork chops or fillet, cut into large cubes	3lb. pork chops or tenderloin, cut into large cubes
8 garlic cloves, crushed	8 garlic cloves, crushed
250ml./8fl.oz. wine vinegar	1 cup wine vinegar
350ml./12fl.oz. water	1½ cups water
2 tsp. soya sauce	2 tsp. soy sauce
black pepper	black pepper
4 Tbs. vegetable oil	4 Tbs. vegetable oil

Put all the ingredients except the oil into a large saucepan and bring to the boil. Cover, reduce the heat to low and simmer gently for 1¼ to 1½ hours, or until the pork is tender. Remove the pork from the pan and set aside. Boil the liquid rapidly until it has reduced by half. Remove from the heat and keep hot.

Meanwhile, heat the oil in a large frying-pan. When it is very hot, add the pork pieces and fry them until they are evenly browned. Transfer them to a serving bowl. Strain over the cooking liquid and serve at once.
Serves 6
Preparation and cooking time: 2 hours

BARBECUED SPARERIBS

(Singapore)

Metric/Imperial	American
1½kg./3lb. American-style spareribs, cut into 2in. pieces	3lb. spareribs, cut into 2-rib serving pieces
salt and pepper	salt and pepper
3 Tbs. soya sauce	3 Tbs. soy sauce
2 Tbs. clear honey	2 Tbs. clear honey
2 tsp. brown sugar	2 tsp. brown sugar
3 Tbs. hoi sin sauce	3 Tbs. hoi sin sauce
2 Tbs. wine vinegar	2 Tbs. wine vinegar
1 Tbs. dry sherry	1 Tbs. dry sherry
1 small onion, chopped	1 small onion, chopped
3 Tbs. chicken stock	3 Tbs. chicken stock
½ tsp. 5-spice powder	½ tsp. 5-spice powder
400g./14oz. tin Chinese plum sauce	14oz. can Chinese plum sauce

Rub the spareribs all over with salt and pepper and arrange them in a shallow dish. Mix all the remaining ingredients, except the plum sauce, together, and pour over the spareribs, basting them well. Set aside to marinate at room temperature for 1 hour, basting occasionally.

Preheat the oven to hot 220°C (Gas Mark 7, 425°F). Remove the spareribs from the liquid and pat dry on kitchen towels. Reserve the marinating liquid. Arrange the ribs in a roasting pan and put into the oven for 30 minutes. Remove from the oven and pour off the fat. Stir in the marinating liquid, basting the ribs thoroughly and return the pan to the oven. Reduce the oven temperature to moderate 180°C (Gas Mark 4, 350°F) and roast the ribs for 1 hour, basting occasionally, or until they are golden brown and crisp. Remove from the oven, and transfer to a serving plate. Strain the cooking liquid and warm it with the plum sauce gently over low heat, stirring occasionally. Pour over the ribs and baste gently until they are thoroughly mixed. Serve at once.

Serves 6-8
Preparation and cooking time: 2½ hours

WETHA HIN LAY

(Pork Curry with Mango)   (Burma)

Metric/Imperial	American
2 medium onions, chopped	2 medium onions, chopped
3 garlic cloves, crushed	3 garlic cloves, crushed
4cm./1½in. piece of fresh root ginger, peeled and chopped	1½in. piece of fresh green ginger, peeled and chopped
1 tsp. ground chilli powder	1 tsp. ground chilli powder
1 tsp. turmeric	1 tsp. turmeric
50ml./2fl. oz. sesame oil	¼ cup sesame oil
1kg./2lb. lean pork, cubed	2 lb. lean pork, cubed
1 Tbs. tamarind	1 Tbs. tamarind
50ml./2fl. oz. boiling water	¼ cup boiling water
1 Tbs. lemon juice	1 Tbs. lemon juice
2 Tbs. mango pickle	2 Tbs. mango pickle
GARNISH	GARNISH
1 fresh mango, stoned and sliced	1 fresh mango, pitted and sliced
2 Tbs. chopped coriander leaves	2 Tbs. chopped coriander leaves

Put the onions, garlic and ginger into a blender and blend to a smooth purée. Stir the chilli powder and turmeric into the spice mixture.

Heat the oil in a large saucepan. When it is hot, add the spice mixture and stir-fry over low heat for 5 minutes. Add the pork cubes and continue to fry until they are evenly browned. Reduce the heat to low and cover the pan. Simmer the pork for 30 minutes.

Meanwhile, put the tamarind into a bowl and pour over the boiling water. Set aside until it is cool. Put the contents of the bowl through a strainer into a second bowl, pressing as much of the pulp through as possible.

Stir the tamarind liquid, lemon juice and mango pickle into the saucepan, re-cover and continue to simmer the mixture for a further 1 hour, or until the pork is cooked through and tender.

Transfer the mixture to a warmed serving dish and garnish with the mango slices and coriander leaves before serving.

Serves 6
Preparation and cooking time: 1¾ hours

WETHANI

(Golden Pork)   (Burma)
The amounts of garlic and ginger are not a mistake – they reflect Burmese taste and are also supposed to 'preserve' the pork!

Metric/Imperial	American
3 onions, finely chopped	3 onions, finely chopped
12 garlic cloves, crushed	12 garlic cloves, crushed
175g./6oz. fresh root ginger, peeled and chopped	1 cup fresh green ginger, peeled and chopped
1½kg./3lb. lean pork, cubed	3lb. lean pork, cubed
salt	salt
2 Tbs. vinegar	2 Tbs. vinegar
50ml./2fl.oz. vegetable oil	¼ cup vegetable oil
1 tsp. hot chilli powder	1 tsp. hot chilli powder

Put the onions, garlic and ginger into a blender and blend to a paste. Put the paste into a strainer or cheesecloth and squeeze gently over a bowl to extract as much juice as possible.

Put the liquid into a large saucepan with the pork, salt, vinegar, oil and chilli powder and bring to the boil. Cover, reduce the heat to low and simmer the pork for 2 hours, or until it is very tender. (You may have to add a tablespoon or two of water during the cooking period if the mixture becomes too dry.) The dish should be 'golden' at the end of cooking, as the translation of its name suggests.
Serves 8
Preparation and cooking time: 2¼ hours

PORK SATE

(Indonesia)

Metric/Imperial	American
½kg./1lb. pork fillet, cut into small cubes	1lb. pork tenderloin, cut into small cubes
MARINADE	MARINADE
3 Tbs. dark soya sauce	3 Tbs. dark soy sauce
2 dried red chillis, crumbled or 1 tsp. sambal ulek	2 dried red chillis, crumbled or 1 tsp. sambal ulek
2 garlic cloves, crushed	2 garlic cloves, crushed
1 Tbs. water	1 Tbs. water
½ tsp. laos powder	½ tsp. laos powder
SAUCE	SAUCE
1 small onion, chopped	1 small onion, chopped
2 garlic cloves, crushed	2 garlic cloves, crushed
2 dried red chillis, crumbled or 1 tsp. sambal ulek	2 dried red chillis, crumbled or 1 tsp. sambal ulek
1 tsp. blachan (dried shrimp paste)	1 tsp. blachan (dried shrimp paste)
1 tsp. chopped lemon grass or grated lemon rind	1 tsp. chopped lemon grass or grated lemon rind
2 tsp. soft brown sugar	2 tsp. soft brown sugar
3 Tbs. peanut oil	3 Tbs. peanut oil
1 Tbs. soya sauce	1 Tbs. soy sauce
2 tsp. lemon juice	2 tsp. lemon juice
4 Tbs. peanut butter	4 Tbs. peanut butter
250ml./8fl.oz. coconut milk	1 cup coconut milk

Combine all the marinade ingredients in a shallow bowl. Add the pork pieces and marinate for 30 minutes, basting occasionally. Thread the pork on to skewers and reserve the marinade.

Preheat the grill (broiler) to moderately high. Arrange the skewers on the rack of the grill (broiler) and grill (broil) for 20 minutes, turning and basting occasionally with the marinade, or until the pork is cooked through.

To make the sauce, combine the onion, garlic, chillis, blachan, lemon grass and sugar in a blender. Heat the oil in a saucepan. When it is hot, add the spice paste and fry for 2 minutes, stirring constantly. Add all the remaining ingredients and combine thoroughly. Bring to the boil. Remove from the heat.

To serve, pour the sauce into a shallow serving bowl and arrange the skewers across.

Serves 4
Preparation and cooking time: 1 hour

MARINATED PORK CHOPS

(Malaysia)

Metric/Imperial	American
2 garlic cloves, crushed	2 garlic cloves, crushed
1 Tbs. crushed coriander seeds	1 Tbs. crushed coriander seeds
8 crushed peppercorns	8 crushed peppercorns
3 Tbs. soya sauce	3 Tbs. soy sauce
1 tsp. soft brown sugar	1 tsp. soft brown sugar
4 loin pork chops	4 loin pork chops

Mix all the ingredients except the chops together in a shallow dish. Put in the chops and coat well. Cover and set aside for 30 minutes, basting the chops occasionally.

Preheat the grill (broiler) to moderately high. Transfer the chops to the rack of the grill (broiler) and reserve the marinade. Grill (broil) the chops for 2 minutes. Reduce the heat to moderate and grill (broil) for 8 to 10 minutes on each side, basting occasionally with the marinating liquid.

Serve at once.

Serves 4
Preparation and cooking time: 1 hour

Easy to make – and even easier to eat – are Marinated Pork Chops, a satisfying dish from Malaysia. Serve with bean sprouts or perhaps mashed potatoes for a filling meal.

CHICKEN

HOT & SOUR CHICKEN, PENANG STYLE

(Malaysia)

Metric/Imperial	American
4 Tbs. vegetable oil	4 Tbs. vegetable oil
3 medium onions, finely chopped	3 medium onions, finely chopped
2 garlic cloves, crushed	2 garlic cloves, crushed
2 red or green chillis, finely chopped	2 red or green chillis, finely chopped
1 Tbs. soft brown sugar	1 Tbs. soft brown sugar
8 chicken pieces	8 chicken pieces
3 Tbs. dark soya sauce	3 Tbs. dark soy sauce
3 Tbs. wine vinegar	3 Tbs. wine vinegar
2 Tbs. water	2 Tbs. water
½ tsp. salt	½ tsp. salt

Heat the oil in a deep frying-pan. When it is hot, add the onions, garlic and chillis and fry for 5 minutes, stirring occasionally. Stir in the sugar and fry until the onions are golden brown.

Add the chicken pieces and fry for 8 minutes, turning frequently, or until they are deeply browned. Stir in the remaining ingredients and bring to the boil. Cover, reduce the heat to low and simmer for 15 minutes. Uncover the pan, increase the heat to moderate and cook the chicken for 25 to 30 minutes, or until it is cooked through.

Serve at once.
Serves 8
Preparation and cooking time: 1 hour

SOY SAUCE CHICKEN

(Indonesia)

Metric/Imperial	American
1 tsp. salt	1 tsp. salt
3 Tbs. wine vinegar	3 Tbs. wine vinegar
1 Tbs. soft brown sugar	1 Tbs. soft brown sugar
1 x 1½kg./3lb. chicken, cut into 12 serving pieces	1 x 3lb. chicken, cut into 12 serving pieces
2 Tbs. peanut or coconut oil	2 Tbs. peanut or coconut oil
SAUCE	SAUCE
1 onion, finely chopped	1 onion, finely chopped
1 green chilli, seeded and finely chopped	1 green chilli, seeded and finely chopped
2 garlic cloves	2 garlic cloves
250ml./8fl.oz. water	1 cup water
1 Tbs. wine vinegar	1 Tbs. wine vinegar
2 Tbs. soya sauce	2 Tbs. soy sauce
1 Tbs. sugar	1 Tbs. sugar
4 medium tomatoes, blanched, peeled, seeded and chopped	4 medium tomatoes, blanched, peeled, seeded and chopped

Combine the salt, vinegar and sugar in a bowl. Toss the chicken pieces in the mixture and set aside for 30 minutes.

Meanwhile, prepare the sauce. Put all the ingredients, except the tomatoes, in a blender and blend until smooth. Pour into a large saucepan and set aside.

Heat the oil in a large frying-pan. When it is hot, add the chicken pieces and fry until they are golden brown all over. Using tongs, transfer to kitchen towels to drain.

Set the pan containing the sauce over moderate heat and bring to the boil. Add the chicken pieces and tomatoes and reduce the heat to low. Cover and simmer for 20 to 25 minutes, or until the chicken is cooked through. Uncover and simmer for a further 10 minutes, or until about a third of the liquid has evaporated.

Transfer the mixture to a warmed serving dish and serve at once.

Serves 6
Preparation and cooking time: 1½ hours

OPAR AYAM

(Chicken in Coconut Gravy)   (Indonesia)

Metric/Imperial	American
3 garlic cloves, crushed	3 garlic cloves, crushed
5cm./2in. piece of fresh root ginger, peeled and chopped	2in. piece of fresh green ginger, peeled and chopped
2 red chillis, chopped	2 red chillis, chopped
3 candle or brazil nuts, chopped	3 candle or brazil nuts, chopped
1 Tbs. ground coriander	1 Tbs. ground coriander
1 tsp. ground cumin	1 tsp. ground cumin
½ tsp. ground fennel	½ tsp. ground fennel
½ tsp. laos powder	½ tsp. laos powder
5 Tbs. peanut oil	5 Tbs. peanut oil
2 medium onions, sliced	2 medium onions, sliced
1 x 2kg./4lb. chicken, cut into serving pieces	1 x 4lb. chicken, cut into serving pieces
1 tsp. chopped lemon grass or grated lemon rind	1 tsp. chopped lemon grass or grated lemon rind
600ml./1 pint thick coconut milk	2½ cups thick coconut milk
2 curry leaves (optional)	2 curry leaves (optional)
1 tsp. sugar	1 tsp. sugar

Put the garlic, ginger, chillis and nuts into a blender and blend to a paste. Transfer to a mixing bowl and stir in the coriander, cumin, fennel and laos powder until they are well mixed. Add about 1 tablespoon of the peanut oil, or a little more if necessary, to blend the mixture to a smooth, thick paste and set aside.

Heat the remaining oil in a large, deep frying-pan. When it is hot, add the onions and fry, stirring occasionally, until they are soft. Add the spice paste and stir-fry for 2 minutes. Add the chicken pieces and baste with the spice mixture until they are thoroughly coated. Stir in the lemon grass or rind and half the coconut milk, and bring to the boil. Reduce the heat to low, cover the pan and simmer for 30 minutes.

Stir in the curry leaves and sugar, then pour over the remaining coconut milk and bring to the boil. Reduce the heat to low and simmer the mixture, uncovered, for 20 to 30 minutes, or until the chicken pieces are cooked through and tender.

Serve at once.

Serves 4–6
Preparation and cooking time: 1¼ hours

TIMOLA

(Chicken Stew)   (The Philippines)

Pawpaw or papaya can be difficult to find in the West; if this is so, mango or guava can be substituted.

Metric/Imperial	American
50g./2oz. vegetable fat	4 Tbs. vegetable fat
1 medium onion, sliced	1 medium onion, sliced
2 garlic cloves, crushed	2 garlic cloves, crushed
4cm./1½in. piece of fresh root ginger, peeled and chopped	1½in. piece of fresh green ginger, peeled and chopped
1 x 1½kg./3lb. chicken, cut into serving pieces	1 x 3lb. chicken, cut into serving pieces
300ml./10fl.oz. water	1¼ cups water
1 pawpaw, peeled and finely chopped	1 pawpaw, peeled and finely chopped
225g./8oz. spinach leaves, chopped	1⅓ cups chopped spinach leaves

Melt the fat in a large saucepan. Add the onion, garlic and ginger and fry, stirring occasionally, until the onion is soft. Add the chicken pieces and fry gently until they are browned all over. Pour over the water and bring to the boil. Reduce the heat to low, cover the pan and simmer for 45 minutes to 1 hour, or until the chicken is cooked through and tender.

Stir in the pawpaw and spinach and cook for a further 10 minutes. Serve at once.
Serves 4
Preparation and cooking time: 1½ hours

SATAY AYAM

(Chicken Sate)   (Indonesia)

Metric/Imperial	American
2 Tbs. soft brown sugar	2 Tbs. soft brown sugar
50ml./2fl.oz. dark treacle	¼ cup molasses
125ml./4fl.oz. dark soy sauce	½ cup dark soy sauce
2 garlic cloves, crushed	2 garlic cloves, crushed
juice of ½ lemon	juice of ½ lemon
2 Tbs. groundnut oil	2 Tbs. groundnut oil
3 chicken breasts	3 chicken breasts
SAUCE	SAUCE
225g./8oz. unsalted peanuts, shelled	1⅓ cups unsalted peanuts, shelled
2 red chillis or 1 tsp. sambal ulek	2 red chillis or 1 tsp. sambal ulek
3 garlic cloves	3 garlic cloves
1 tsp. salt	1 tsp. salt
1 onion, coarsely chopped	1 onion, coarsely chopped
50ml./2fl.oz. groundnut oil	¼ cup groundnut oil
75-125ml./3-4fl.oz. water	⅓-½ cup water
1 Tbs. soft brown sugar mixed with 2 Tbs. dark soy sauce	1 Tbs. soft brown sugar mixed with 2 Tbs. dark soy sauce
1-2 Tbs. lemon juice	1-2 Tbs. lemon juice

Mix the sugar, treacle (molasses) and soy sauce together in a small bowl. Stir in the garlic, lemon juice and oil and set aside.

Skin and bone the chicken breasts, then cut the meat into 1½cm./¾in. cubes. Thread the cubes on to skewers and arrange the skewers in a shallow dish. Pour over the soy sauce mixture and set aside to marinate at room temperature for 1 hour, basting occasionally. Turn the skewers in the marinade from time to time.

Preheat the grill (broiler) to high.

To make the sauce, put the peanuts in the grill (broiler) pan and grill (broil) them for 2 to 3 minutes, turning occasionally. Remove from the heat and gently rub them between your hands to remove the skins. Put the peanuts in a grinder or blender with the chillis or sambal ulek, garlic, salt, onion and 2 tablespoons of the groundnut oil. Blend to a thick paste, adding enough of the water to prevent the blender from sticking. Remove the paste from the blender, put in a bowl and set aside.

Heat the remaining oil in a saucepan. When it is hot, add the nut paste. Reduce the heat to moderately low and fry the paste for 3 minutes, stirring constantly. Stir in the remaining water and simmer gently for 5 minutes, or until it is thick and smooth. Remove from the heat and stir in the soy sauce mixture and lemon juice. Taste and add more salt and lemon if necessary. Keep hot while you cook the chicken.

Arrange the skewers on the rack of the grill (broiler). Grill (broil) the chicken for 5 minutes, turning occasionally, or until the cubes are cooked through and tender.

Remove from the heat and arrange the skewers on a warmed serving platter, or across a serving bowl. Serve at once, with the sauce.

Serves 4-6
Preparation and cooking time: 1½ hours

MANGO CHICKEN

(Malaysia)

Metric/Imperial	American
1 x 2kg./4lb. chicken, cut into serving pieces	1 x 4lb. chicken, cut into serving pieces
salt and pepper	salt and pepper
3 Tbs. peanut oil	3 Tbs. peanut oil
1 large onion, thinly sliced	1 large onion, thinly sliced
1 mango, peeled, stoned and sliced	1 mango, peeled, pitted and sliced
1 tsp. chopped lemon grass or grated lemon rind	1 tsp. chopped lemon grass or grated lemon rind
¼ tsp. ground coriander	¼ tsp. ground coriander
¼ tsp. ground cinnamon	¼ tsp. ground cinnamon
250ml./8fl.oz. chicken stock	1 cup chicken stock
250ml./8fl.oz. single cream	1 cup light cream
2 tsp. flour, mixed to a paste with 1 Tbs. lemon juice and 1 Tbs. water	2 tsp. flour, mixed to a paste with 1 Tbs. lemon juice and 1 Tbs. water

Preheat the oven to fairly hot 190°C (Gas Mark 5, 375°F).

Rub the chicken pieces all over with the salt and pepper, then set aside.

Heat the oil in a large frying-pan. When it is hot, add the chicken pieces and fry, stirring occasionally, until they are evenly browned. Using a slotted spoon, transfer

the chicken pieces to a flameproof casserole. Set aside.

Add the onion to the frying-pan and fry until it is soft. Using the slotted spoon, transfer the onion to the casserole.

Add the mango slices to the frying-pan and fry, turning once, for 4 minutes. Stir in the lemon grass or rind, coriander, cinnamon and stock to the pan and bring to the boil, stirring constantly. Pour over the chicken and onion mixture in the casserole.

Cover the casserole and put into the oven. Bake for 1¼ hours, or until the chicken is cooked through and tender. Remove from the oven and, using tongs or a slotted spoon, transfer the chicken pieces to a warmed serving dish. Keep hot while you finish the sauce.

Bring the casserole liquid to the boil. Reduce the heat to low and stir in the cream and flour mixture. Cook the sauce, stirring constantly, until it is hot but not boiling and has thickened.

Remove the casserole from the heat and pour the sauce over the chicken pieces. Serve at once.

Serves 4
Preparation and cooking time: 2 hours

This dish combines two favourite South-East Asian foods: mangoes and chicken. Mango Chicken is smooth, rich and spicy, without being hot.

AYAM BALI

(Balinese Fried Chicken) (Indonesia)

Metric/Imperial	American
1 medium onion, chopped	1 medium onion, chopped
2 garlic cloves, crushed	2 garlic cloves, crushed
2½cm./1in. piece of fresh root ginger, peeled and chopped	1in. piece of fresh root ginger, peeled and chopped
2 red chillis, chopped	2 red chillis, chopped
4 candle or brazil nuts, chopped	4 candle or brazil nuts, chopped
250ml./8fl.oz. coconut milk or water	1 cup coconut milk or water
50ml./2fl.oz. peanut oil	¼ cup peanut oil
4 large chicken pieces	4 large chicken pieces
1 Tbs. soya sauce	1 Tbs. soy sauce
1 tsp. soft brown sugar	1 tsp. soft brown sugar
1 tsp. wine vinegar	1 tsp. wine vinegar

Put the onion, garlic, ginger, chillis and nuts into a blender with 2 tablespoons of the coconut milk or water and blend to a smooth purée.

Heat the oil in a large, deep frying-pan. When it is hot, add the chicken pieces and fry for 8 to 10 minutes, or until they are evenly browned. Using tongs or a slotted spoon, transfer the chicken pieces to a plate and keep hot.

Add the purée mixture to the frying-pan and stir-fry for 5 minutes. Stir in the remaining coconut milk or water, the soy sauce, sugar and vinegar and bring to the boil. Add the chicken pieces to the pan and baste them thoroughly with the liquid. Reduce the heat to low and simmer the chicken, uncovered, for 30 to 40 minutes, or until the pieces are cooked through and tender.

Transfer the mixture to a warmed serving dish and serve at once.
Serves 4
Preparation and cooking time: 1¼ hours

KAUKSWE-HIN

(Curried Chicken with Noodles) (Burma)

Metric/Imperial	American
½ tsp. hot chilli powder	½ tsp. hot chilli powder
1 tsp. turmeric	1 tsp. turmeric
½ tsp. ground cumin	½ tsp. ground cumin
3 Tbs. sesame oil	3 Tbs. sesame oil
4 garlic cloves, crushed	4 garlic cloves, crushed
2½cm./1in. piece of fresh root ginger, peeled and chopped	1in. piece of fresh green ginger, peeled and chopped
4 onions, chopped	4 onions, chopped
½ tsp. chopped lemon grass or grated lemon rind	½ tsp. chopped lemon grass or grated lemon rind
1 x 2kg./4lb. chicken, cut into serving pieces	1 x 4lb. chicken, cut into serving pieces
450ml./15fl.oz. thin coconut milk	2 cups thin coconut milk
300ml./10fl.oz. thick coconut milk	1¼ cups thick coconut milk
salt	salt
½ tsp. lime or lemon juice	½ tsp. lime or lemon juice
½ kg./1lb. fine noodles or vermicelli	1lb. fine noodles or vermicelli

Kaukswe-Hin, a delectable mixture of chicken curry and noodles topped by a variety of garnishes, is almost the Burmese national dish. It is served here with Than That, a popular cucumber pickle.

GARNISH

4 spring onions, chopped
2 Tbs. chopped coriander leaves
6 lemon wedges
3 hard-boiled eggs, chopped

GARNISH

4 scallions, chopped
2 Tbs. chopped coriander leaves
6 lemon wedges
3 hard-cooked eggs, chopped

Mix together the chilli powder, turmeric and cumin and set aside.

Heat the oil in a large saucepan. When it is hot, add the garlic, ginger and onions and fry, stirring occasionally, until the onions are soft. Stir in the spice mixture and fry for 1 minute, stirring constantly. Add the chicken pieces and fry until they are lightly browned all over. Pour over the thin coconut milk and bring to the boil. Reduce the heat to low and simmer the mixture, uncovered, for 1 to $1\frac{1}{4}$ hours, or until the chicken pieces are tender. Stir in the thick coconut milk, salt and lime or lemon juice. Simmer for 5 minutes.

Meanwhile, cook the noodles in boiling salted water for 5 minutes. Drain and keep them hot. Arrange the garnishes in separate, small bowls.

To serve, put the chicken curry in one large serving bowl, and divide the noodles among individual bowls. Each diner should ladle the chicken and gravy over the noodles and sprinkle over the garnishes as required.

Serves 4-6
Preparation and cooking time: 2 hours

AJAM GORENG

(Spicy Fried Chicken)   (Indonesia)

Metric/Imperial	American
1 x 1½kg./3lb. chicken, cut into 12 or 15 pieces	1 x 3lb. chicken, cut into 12 or 15 pieces
25g./1oz. tamarind	1oz. tamarind
125ml./4fl. oz. boiling water	½ cup boiling water
2 garlic cloves, crushed	2 garlic cloves, crushed
2 tsp. ground coriander	2 tsp. ground coriander
1 tsp. ground ginger	1 tsp. ground ginger
1 Tbs. wine vinegar or lemon juice	1 Tbs. wine vinegar or lemon juice
1 tsp. soft brown sugar	1 tsp. soft brown sugar
50g./2oz. flour	½ cup flour
vegetable oil for deep-frying	vegetable oil for deep-frying

Put the chicken pieces into a large, shallow dish and set aside.

Put the tamarind into a bowl and pour over the boiling water. Set aside until it is cool. Put the contents of the bowl through a strainer into the dish containing the chicken, pressing as much of the pulp through as possible.

Combine all the remaining ingredients, except the flour and oil, beating until they are thoroughly combined. Stir them into the dish containing the chicken until the mixture is blended and all the pieces are well coated. Put into the refrigerator to marinate for at least 8 hours, or overnight. Remove from the dish.

Fill a large deep-frying pan about one-third full with oil and heat until it is very hot. Dip the chicken pieces into the flour, shaking off any excess flour. Carefully lower the pieces into the oil, a few at a time, and deep-fry for 5 to 8 minutes, or until they are cooked through and golden brown. Remove from the oil and drain on kitchen towels. Serve hot.

Serves 4
Preparation and cooking time: $8\frac{1}{2}$ hours

FRIED CHICKEN WITH MUSHROOMS

(Cambodia)

Metric/Imperial	American
50ml./2fl.oz. peanut oil	¼ cup peanut oil
3 garlic cloves, crushed	3 garlic cloves, crushed
5cm./2in. piece of fresh root ginger, peeled and chopped	2in. piece of fresh green ginger, peeled and chopped
1 x 1½kg./3lb. chicken, cut into small pieces	1 x 3lb. chicken, cut into small pieces
8 dried Chinese mushrooms, soaked in cold water for 30 minutes, drained, stalks removed and sliced	8 dried Chinese mushrooms, soaked in cold water for 30 minutes, drained, stalks removed and sliced
1 Tbs. sugar	1 Tbs. sugar
2 Tbs. vinegar	2 Tbs. vinegar
2 Tbs. fish sauce	2 Tbs. fish sauce
175ml./6fl.oz. water	¾ cup water
1 Tbs. chopped coriander leaves	1 Tbs. chopped coriander leaves

Heat the oil in a large saucepan. When it is hot, add the garlic and ginger and stir-fry for 2 minutes. Add the chicken and cook for 8 to 10 minutes, stirring occasionally. Stir in all the remaining ingredients, except the coriander, and stir-fry for 10 minutes, or until the chicken is cooked through.

Transfer the mixture to a warmed serving bowl and garnish with the coriander before serving.
Serves 4
Preparation and cooking time: 50 minutes

KAI TOM KHA

(Chicken with Laos Powder)   (Thailand)

Metric/Imperial	American
1 x 2kg./4lb. chicken, cut into serving pieces	1 x 4lb. chicken, cut into serving pieces
450ml./15fl.oz. thin coconut milk	2 cups thin coconut milk
4 tsp. laos powder	4 tsp. laos powder
2 tsp. chopped lemon grass or grated lemon rind	2 tsp. chopped lemon grass or grated lemon rind
1 green chilli, finely chopped	1 green chilli, finely chopped
250ml./8fl.oz. thick coconut milk	1 cup thick coconut milk
1 tsp. fish sauce	1 tsp. fish sauce
1 Tbs. lemon juice	1 Tbs. lemon juice
2 Tbs. chopped coriander leaves	2 Tbs. chopped coriander leaves

Put the chicken pieces into a large saucepan and pour over the thin coconut milk. Stir in the laos powder, chopped lemon grass or lemon rind and chilli and bring to the boil. Cover the pan, reduce the heat to low and simmer the mixture gently for 30 minutes. Uncover and continue to simmer for a further 15 to 20 minutes, or until the chicken pieces are cooked through and tender.

Pour over the thick coconut milk and bring to the boil. Reduce the heat to low and simmer for 5 minutes. Stir in the fish sauce and lemon juice.

Transfer the mixture to a warmed serving bowl and garnish with the chopped coriander leaves before serving.

Serves 4-6
Preparation and cooking time: 1¼ hours

GRILLED (BROILED) CHICKEN

(Malaysia)

Metric/Imperial	American
25 blanched almonds,	25 blanched almonds
2 green chillis	2 green chillis
3 garlic cloves	3 garlic cloves
1 tsp. chopped lemon grass or grated lemon rind	1 tsp. chopped lemon grass or grated lemon rind
2 tsp. turmeric	2 tsp. turmeric
1 Tbs. coriander seeds	1 Tbs. coriander seeds
½ tsp. hot chilli powder	½ tsp. hot chilli powder
1 tsp. sugar	1 tsp. sugar
½ tsp. laos powder	½ tsp. laos powder
½ tsp. salt	½ tsp. salt
juice of 1 lemon	juice of 1 lemon
3 Tbs. vegetable oil	3 Tbs. vegetable oil
300ml./10fl.oz. coconut milk	1¼ cups coconut milk
1 x 2kg./4lb. chicken, cut into quarters	1 x 4lb. chicken, cut into quarters

Put the almonds, spices, salt and lemon juice into a blender and blend, adding a spoonful or two of water, until the mixture becomes a thick paste. Scrape into a cup and set aside.

Heat the oil in a large saucepan. When it is hot, add the spice paste and fry for 5 minutes, stirring constantly. Stir in the coconut milk and chicken pieces and bring to the boil. Cover, reduce the heat to low and simmer for 40 minutes, or until the chicken is just cooked and the liquid is thick and nearly all evaporated. Cook uncovered for the last 10 minutes.

Preheat the grill (broiler) to high. Put the chicken pieces on the rack in the grill (broiler) and grill (broil) for 3 to 4 minutes on each side, or until they are golden brown, basting occasionally with the reserved cooking liquid.

Serve at once.

Serves 6
Preparation and cooking time: 1 hour

KAPITAN CURRY

(Singapore)

Metric/Imperial	American
4 Tbs. vegetable oil	4 Tbs. vegetable oil
2 medium onions, finely chopped	2 medium onions, finely chopped
3 garlic cloves, crushed	3 garlic cloves, crushed

4cm./1½in. piece of fresh root ginger, peeled and chopped	1½in. piece of fresh green ginger, peeled and chopped
6 green chillis, 2 finely chopped and 4 whole	6 green chillis, 2 finely chopped and 4 whole
2 Tbs. ground coriander	2 Tbs. ground coriander
2 tsp. ground cumin	2 tsp. ground cumin
1 whole star anise, crushed	1 whole star anise, crushed
1 tsp. turmeric	1 tsp. turmeric
½ tsp. grated nutmeg	½ tsp. grated nutmeg
½ tsp. ground cinnamon	½ tsp. ground cinnamon
½ tsp. ground cardamom	½ tsp. ground cardamom
8 chicken pieces	8 chicken pieces
600ml./1 pint coconut milk	2½ cups coconut milk
1 tsp. salt	1 tsp. salt

Heat the oil in a large saucepan. When it is hot, add the onions, garlic, ginger and chopped chillis and fry, stirring occasionally, until the onions are golden brown. Stir in the spices and fry for 5 minutes, stirring constantly. If the mixture becomes too dry, add a spoonful or two of water. Add the chicken pieces and turn over in the spice mixture. Fry for 5 minutes, turning occasionally.

Pour over the coconut milk and add the salt and whole chillis. Cover, reduce the heat to low and simmer the curry for 45 minutes to 1 hour, or until the chicken is cooked through.

Transfer the chicken pieces to a serving bowl and pour over the sauce. Serve at once.

Serves 8
Preparation and cooking time: 1¼ hours

Kapitan Curry from Singapore is a delightful chicken dish with a coconut-flavoured gravy. Serve with rice and a variety of chutneys for a superb meal.

PAPER WRAPPED CHICKEN

(Singapore)

This dish reflects the very strong Chinese influence still present in Singapore and Malay food – it is, in fact, a standard dish in many ethnic Chinese restaurants as well as Singapore and Malaysian ones. In the Far East the chicken pieces would undoubtedly be deep-fried in rice paper, which is edible, and these can be obtained from Chinese general stores. However, if they are not available, greaseproof or waxed paper can be used instead.

Metric/Imperial	American
2 large chicken breasts, skinned, boned and cut into bite-sized pieces	2 large chicken breasts, skinned, boned and cut into bite-sized pieces
rice or greaseproof paper	rice or waxed paper
8 dried mushrooms, soaked in cold water for 30 minutes, drained and chopped	8 dried mushrooms, soaked in cold water for 30 minutes, drained and chopped
4 spring onions, chopped	4 scallions, chopped
4cm./1½in. piece of fresh root ginger, peeled and thinly sliced	1½in. piece of fresh green ginger, peeled and thinly sliced
3 Tbs. frozen green peas, thawed	3 Tbs. frozen green peas, thawed
vegetable oil for deep-frying	vegetable oil for deep-frying
MARINADE	MARINADE
1½ Tbs. oyster sauce	1½ Tbs. oyster sauce
1 Tbs. sesame oil	1 Tbs. sesame oil
1 Tbs. rice wine or sherry	1 Tbs. rice wine or sherry
½ tsp. sugar	½ tsp. sugar
¼ tsp. ground ginger	¼ tsp. ground ginger

First, make the marinade. Put all the ingredients into a shallow bowl and mix until they are thoroughly blended. Add the chicken pieces to the bowl and stir them gently until they are thoroughly basted. Set aside at room temperature for 1 hour, turning and basting from time to time.

Cut the paper into squares about 15cm./6in. in diameter. Arrange a little of the filling just off centre (see the sketch below) and carefully add a little mushroom, spring onion (scallion), ginger and peas to the filling. Fold up the paper, as explained in the sketch so that the filling is completely enclosed, envelope fashion.

Fill a large deep-frying pan about one-third full with vegetable oil and heat until it is hot. Carefully lower the 'packets' into the oil, two or three at a time, and fry for 3 to 5 minutes, turning occasionally. Remove from the oil and drain on kitchen towels.

To serve, if using rice paper serve the packets to be eaten, paper and all; if using greaseproof or waxed paper, open the packets on individual serving plates and serve at once.

Serves 4

Preparation and cooking time: 1¾ hours

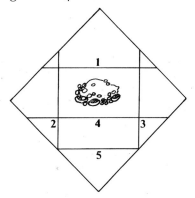

DUCK

GREEN DUCK CURRY

(Thailand)

This dish can be made with either duck or chicken; the 'green' part of the title comes from the greenish tinge of the curry paste, which is effected by using green rather than red chillis and coriander leaves. The root of the coriander plant is traditionally used in Thailand as an ingredient in this curry paste but since it is virtually unobtainable in the West, the leaf has been substituted.

Metric/Imperial	American
300ml./10fl.oz. thin coconut milk	1¼ cups thin coconut milk
1 x 3kg./6lb. duck, cut into 8-10 serving pieces	1 x 6lb. duck, cut into 8-10 serving pieces
1 Tbs. fish sauce	1 Tbs. fish sauce
2 Tbs. chopped coriander leaves	2 Tbs. chopped coriander leaves
300ml./10fl.oz. thick coconut milk	1¼ cups thick coconut milk
CURRY PASTE	CURRY PASTE
3 spring onions, green part included, chopped	3 scallions, green part included, chopped
2 garlic cloves, crushed	2 garlic cloves, crushed
3 green chillis, chopped	3 green chillis, chopped
2 tsp. grated lime rind	2 tsp. grated lime rind
1 Tbs. chopped coriander leaves	1 Tbs. chopped coriander leaves
1 tsp. chopped lemon grass or grated lemon rind	1 tsp. chopped lemon grass or grated lemon rind
2 tsp. ground coriander	2 tsp. ground coriander
1 tsp. ground cumin	1 tsp. ground cumin
1 tsp. laos powder	1 tsp. laos powder
salt and pepper	salt and pepper
1 tsp. blachan (dried shrimp paste)	1 tsp. blachan (dried shrimp paste)
½ tsp. turmeric	½ tsp. turmeric

To make the curry paste, put the spring onions (scallions), garlic, chillis, lime rind, coriander leaves and lemon grass or rind into a blender with a little of the thin coconut milk. Blend to a very thick purée. Transfer the purée to a bowl and stir in the remaining curry paste ingredients until all the ingredients are well blended.

Put the remaining thin coconut milk into a large saucepan and bring to the boil. Add the duck pieces and return the mixture to the boil. Reduce the heat to low and simmer for 1 to 1¼ hours, or until the duck is cooked through and tender.

Pour about half of the liquid in the pan with the duck into a second large saucepan and bring to the boil. Stir in the curry paste and fry, stirring frequently, over high heat until the milk has almost evaporated. Reduce the heat to moderate and continue frying the mixture for 3 minutes in the oily milk residue, stirring constantly. Gradually stir in the remaining coconut milk from the pan containing the duck and cook the mixture until it is thick and the oil begins to separate from the liquid.

Add the cooked duck pieces, fish sauce, half the chopped coriander and the thick coconut milk. Bring to the boil and reduce the heat to moderately low. Cook the mixture for 5 minutes, or until the liquid has thickened. Stir in the remaining coriander leaves and simmer for 5 minutes.

Serve at once.

Serves 4–6
Preparation and cooking time: 2 hours

MALAYSIAN DUCK

Metric/Imperial	American
1 Tbs. ground coriander	1 Tbs. ground coriander
2 tsp. ground fenugreek	2 tsp. ground fenugreek
2 tsp. ground cumin	2 tsp. ground cumin
1 tsp. turmeric	1 tsp. turmeric
1 tsp. ground cinnamon	1 tsp. ground cinnamon
½ tsp. ground cardamom	½ tsp. ground cardamom
¼ tsp. grated nutmeg	¼ tsp. grated nutmeg
1 tsp. mild chilli powder	1 tsp. mild chilli powder
salt and pepper	salt and pepper
juice of 1 lemon	juice of 1 lemon
1cm./½in. piece of fresh root ginger, peeled and chopped	½in. piece of fresh green ginger, peeled and chopped
2 small onions, minced	2 small onions, ground
2 garlic cloves, crushed	2 garlic cloves, crushed
125g./4oz. desiccated coconut, soaked in 175ml./6fl.oz. boiling water	½ cup shredded coconut, soaked in ¾ cup boiling water
1 x 2½kg./5lb. duck, split through the breast bone, ribs broken at the backbone and wings and legs tied together	1 x 5lb. duck, split through the breast bone, ribs broken at the backbone and wings and legs tied together

Preheat the oven to fairly hot 190°C (Gas Mark 5, 375°F).

Mix all the spices together in a bowl and add seasoning, lemon juice, ginger, onions, garlic and coconut milk to form a thick paste. Spread the paste over the duck.

Put the duck on a rack in a roasting pan and roast for 1½ hours, basting every 15 minutes or so. Halfway through roasting, turn the duck over. When it is cooked through, baste once more then remove from the oven.

Serve at once.

Serves 4–6
Preparation and cooking time: 1¾ hours

Barbecuing is a very popular method of cooking in Malaysia, and this simple but delicious Malaysian Duck demonstrates why. The duck is first marinated in a spicy coconut paste, then barbecued to crisp perfection.

FISH

IKAN BANDENG

(Baked Spiced Fish)   (Indonesia)

Bandeng is a type of sole, found around the coast of Indonesia. Any type of fish can be substituted however – grey mullet, red snapper, even a large whiting.

Metric/Imperial	American
2 Tbs. vegetable oil	2 Tbs. vegetable oil
1 x 1½kg./3lb. fish, cleaned and gutted	1 x 3lb fish, cleaned and gutted
3 garlic cloves, crushed	3 garlic cloves, crushed
7½cm./3in. piece of fresh root ginger, peeled and minced	3in. piece of fresh green ginger, peeled and minced
3 Tbs. soya sauce	3 Tbs. soy sauce
1½ Tbs. lemon juice	1½ Tbs. lemon juice
3 tsp. dried chillis or sambal ulek	3 tsp. dried chillis or sambal ulek
GARNISH	GARNISH
2 lemons, cut into wedges	2 lemons, cut into wedges
3 Tbs. chopped coriander leaves	3 Tbs. chopped coriander leaves

Preheat the oven to fairly hot 190°C (Gas Mark 5, 375°F).

Make some deep gashes across the fish with a sharp knife. Pour the oil into a roasting pan, then transfer the fish to the pan.

Beat the garlic, ginger, soy sauce, lemon juice and sambal ulek together until they are well blended, then pour over the fish, rubbing the mixture into the flesh and gashes.

Cover with foil then put the roasting pan into the oven. Bake the fish for 25 to 30 minutes, or until the flesh flakes easily.

Remove from the oven and serve at once, garnished with lemon wedges and coriander leaves.

Serves 4-6
Preparation and cooking time: 40 minutes

VIETNAMESE FRIED FISH

Metric/Imperial	American
4 Tbs. cornflour	4 Tbs. cornstarch
salt and pepper	salt and pepper
4 small bream, cleaned and with the eyes removed	4 small porgy, cleaned and with the eyes removed
50ml./2fl.oz. peanut oil	¼ cup peanut oil
nuoc cham (page 92)	nuoc cham (page 92)

Mix the cornflour (cornstarch) with salt and pepper to taste and use to coat the fish lightly. Heat the oil in a large frying-pan. When it is hot, add the fish and fry for 10 to 12 minutes, or until the flesh flakes.

Serve at once, with nuoc cham.

Serves 4
Preparation and cooking time: 15 minutes

FISH FILLETS WITH PINEAPPLE AND GINGER

(Malaysia)

Metric/Imperial	American
2 tsp. turmeric	2 tsp. turmeric
1½ tsp. salt	1½ tsp. salt
700g./1½lb. fish fillets, cut into bite-sized pieces	1½lb. fish fillets, cut into bite-sized pieces
3 Tbs. vegetable oil	3 Tbs. vegetable oil
2 onions, finely chopped	2 onions, finely chopped
4cm./1½in. piece of fresh root ginger, peeled and chopped	1½in. piece of fresh green ginger, peeled and chopped
2 chillis, finely chopped	2 chillis, finely chopped
1 tsp. blachan (dried shrimp paste)	1 tsp. blachan (dried shrimp paste)
1 tsp. ground lemon grass or finely grated lemon rind	1 tsp. ground lemon grass or finely grated lemon rind
1 tsp. sugar	1 tsp. sugar
4 tomatoes, blanched, peeled and chopped	4 tomatoes, blanched, peeled and chopped
1 small pineapple, peeled, cored and cut into chunks	1 small pineapple, peeled, cored and cut into chunks

Mix half the turmeric with 1 teaspoon of salt, then rub over the fish pieces.

Heat the oil in a large frying-pan. When it is hot, add the fish pieces and fry for 2 minutes on each side. Remove the fish to a plate. If necessary, add more oil to the pan to cover the bottom. Add the onions and fry, stirring occasionally, until they are golden brown. Add the ginger, chillis, blachan, lemon grass or rind and remaining turmeric and fry over low heat for 5 minutes, stirring constantly. Stir in the sugar, tomatoes and remaining salt, the pineapple and fish pieces. Cover and simmer for 20 to 25 minutes, or until the fish flakes easily. Serve at once.
Serves 6–8
Preparation and cooking time: 50 minutes

OTAK-OTAK

(Steamed Fish Parcels)   (Malaysia)

In Malaysia banana leaves are used as wrappers for this dish, but foil or any other heatproof wrapping makes a good Western substitute.

Metric/Imperial	American
700g./1½lb. cod or other white fish fillets, skinned and cut into strips	1½lb. cod or other white fish fillets, skinned and cut into strips
SAUCE	SAUCE
2 garlic cloves, crushed	2 garlic cloves, crushed
4 green chillis, finely chopped	4 green chillis, finely chopped
½ tsp. chopped lemon grass or grated lemon rind	½ tsp. chopped lemon grass or grated lemon rind
1 tsp. turmeric	1 tsp. turmeric
salt and pepper	salt and pepper
4 Tbs. desiccated coconut	4 Tbs. shredded coconut
250ml./8fl.oz. thick coconut milk	1 cup thick coconut milk

Pound all the sauce ingredients, except the coconut milk, together until they form a smooth paste. Put the milk into a saucepan and heat until it is hot but not boiling. Remove the pan from the heat and stir in the paste mixture.

Cut out four medium squares of foil. Spread some of the coconut mixture over the bottom of each one, then divide the fish between them. Cover with the remaining coconut mixture. Fold the foil into neat parcels, to enclose the filling completely.

Place the parcels in the top of a double boiler or in a heatproof plate set over a pan of boiling water. Cover and steam for 30 minutes.

Serve straight from the wrapping.
Serves 4
Preparation and cooking time: 45 minutes

IKAN ACHAR

(Vinegar Fish)   (Malaysia)

Metric/Imperial	American
1 onion, chopped	1 onion, chopped
1 garlic clove, crushed	1 garlic clove, crushed
2½cm./1in. piece of fresh root ginger, peeled and chopped	1in. piece of fresh green ginger, peeled and chopped
4 candle or brazil nuts, chopped	4 candle or brazil nuts, chopped
1 tsp. chopped dried red chillis or sambal ulek	1 tsp. chopped dried red chillis or sambal ulek
125ml./4fl.oz. water	½ cup water
50ml./2fl.oz. peanut oil	¼ cup peanut oil
2 Tbs. wine vinegar	2 Tbs. wine vinegar
½ tsp. soft brown sugar	½ tsp. soft brown sugar
½kg./1lb. fish fillets, skinned	1lb. fish fillets, skinned

Put the onion, garlic, ginger, candle or brazil nuts, chillis or sambal ulek into a blender with about 3 tablespoons of the water. Blend to a smooth purée.

Heat the oil in a large frying-pan. When it is hot, add the purée mixture and stir-fry for 3 minutes. Pour over the remaining water, the vinegar and stir in the sugar. Bring to the boil, then reduce the heat to low.

Arrange the fish fillets in the pan and spoon over the sauce to baste them completely. Cover the pan and simmer the fish for 10 to 15 minutes, or until the flesh flakes easily.

Transfer the mixture to a warmed serving dish and serve at once.
Serves 4
Preparation and cooking time: 35 minutes

SAMBAL GORENG SOTONG

(Squid Sambal)   (Malaysia)

Metric/Imperial	American
25g./1oz. tamarind	2 Tbs. tamarind
125ml./4fl.oz. boiling water	½ cup boiling water
4 whole almonds	4 whole almonds
4 dried red chillis, chopped	4 dried red chillis, chopped

2 garlic cloves, crushed
1 small onion, chopped
½ tsp. blachan (dried shrimp paste)
1½ Tbs. peanut oil
½ tsp. chopped lemon grass or
   grated lemon rind
2 tsp. jaggery or soft brown sugar
2 tsp. paprika
4 large squid, cleaned, gutted and
   sliced crosswise

2 garlic cloves, crushed
1 small onion, chopped
½ tsp. blachan (dried shrimp paste)
1½ Tbs. peanut oil
½ tsp. chopped lemon grass or
   grated lemon rind
2 tsp. jaggery or soft brown sugar
2 tsp. paprika
4 large squid, cleaned, gutted and
   sliced crosswise

Put the tamarind into a bowl and pour over the boiling water. Set aside until it is cool. Pour the contents of the bowl through a strainer into a second bowl, pressing as much of the pulp through as possible. Set aside.

Meanwhile, put the almonds, chillis, garlic, onion, blachan and about 1 tablespoon of oil into a blender and blend to a smooth purée.

Heat the remaining oil in a large, deep frying-pan. When it is hot, add the almond mixture and lemon grass or rind and stir-fry for 2 minutes. Add the tamarind water, sugar and paprika and continue to cook for 3 minutes, stirring constantly. Add the squid and cook for 10 to 15 minutes, stirring occasionally, or until the squid is cooked through and tender.

Transfer the mixture to a warmed serving dish and serve at once.

Serves 4-6
Preparation and cooking time: 45 minutes

PLA NUM

(Fish in Red Sauce)   (Thailand)

Metric/Imperial	American
700g./1½lb. fish	1½lb. fish
50ml./2fl. oz. peanut oil	¼ cup peanut oil
1 large onion, chopped	1 large onion, chopped
2 garlic cloves, crushed	2 garlic cloves, crushed
1 red chilli, chopped	1 red chilli, chopped
2 large tomatoes, blanched, peeled and chopped	2 large tomatoes, blanched, peeled and chopped
2 Tbs. tomato purée	2 Tbs. tomato paste
4 Tbs. water	4 Tbs. water
2 Tbs. wine vinegar	2 Tbs. wine vinegar
salt and pepper	salt and pepper
2 Tbs. chopped coriander leaves	2 Tbs. chopped coriander leaves

Clean and cut the fish if you are using a whole one; skin if you are using fillets.

Heat the oil in a large deep frying-pan. When it is hot, add the onion, garlic and chilli and stir-fry for 3 minutes. Add the tomatoes and cook gently until they have pulped. Stir in the tomato purée (paste), water and vinegar, and season to taste. Bring the mixture to the boil, then reduce the heat to low. Simmer, covered, for 10 minutes.

Arrange the fish in the sauce, basting thoroughly. Re-cover the pan and simmer the fish for 10 to 20 minutes, or until the flesh flakes easily. Just before serving, stir in about half of the coriander leaves.

Transfer the mixture to a warmed serving dish and garnish with the remaining coriander leaves before serving.

Serves 4-6
Preparation and cooking time: 1 hour

*Spiced Plaice (Flounder)
The combination of
Chinese and Malay
expertise is demonstrated
beautifully in Spiced
Plaice (Flounder) – fish
marinated in a mixture of
soy sauce, sugar and chilli
powder and
then barbecued.*

SPICED PLAICE (FLOUNDER)

(Malaysia)

Metric/Imperial	American
125ml./4fl.oz. dark soy sauce	$\frac{1}{2}$ cup dark soy sauce
2 Tbs. soft brown sugar	2 Tbs. soft brown sugar
1 tsp. hot chilli powder	1 tsp. hot chilli powder
2 garlic cloves, crushed	2 garlic cloves, crushed
4 plaice, cleaned, gutted and prepared for cooking	4 flounder, cleaned, gutted and prepared for cooking
25g./1oz. butter	2 Tbs. butter
juice of 1 lemon	juice of 1 lemon

Combine the soy sauce, sugar, chilli powder and garlic together. Put the fish in a shallow dish and pour over the soy sauce mixture. Cover and set aside for 1 hour, basting occasionally.

Preheat the grill (broiler) to high.

Arrange the fish on the rack of the grill (broiler) and grill (broil) the fish, turning them once, for 8 to 10 minutes, or until the flesh flakes easily, basting occasionally with the marinade.

Melt the butter in a small saucepan. Stir in the lemon juice and remove from the heat. Carefully transfer the fish to individual plates and discard the remaining marinade.

Pour the melted butter mixture over the fish and serve at once.

Serves 4
Preparation and cooking time: $1\frac{1}{4}$ hours

IKAN GORENG

(Fried Fish in Lime Juice)   (Indonesia)

Ikan Goreng (Fried Fish in Lime Juice) comes from Indonesia and is made here with mackerel. The rich yellow colour is produced by rubbing turmeric over the marinated fish.

Metric/Imperial	American
300ml./10fl.oz. lime juice	1¼ cups lime juice
50ml./2fl.oz. wine vinegar	¼ cup wine vinegar
1 tsp. salt	1 tsp. salt
6 black peppercorns	6 black peppercorns
2 1k x g./2lb. mackerel, filleted	2 x 2lb. mackerel, filleted
1 tsp. turmeric	1 tsp. turmeric
4 Tbs. peanut oil	4 Tbs. peanut oil

Combine the lime juice, vinegar, ½ teaspoon of salt and the peppercorns together in a large, shallow dish. Place the fish in the dish and baste well. Set aside for 1 hour, basting occasionally. Remove from the marinade and dry on kitchen towels. Remove and discard the peppercorns from the marinade and reserve about 50ml./2 fl. oz. (¼ cup).

Rub the fish all over with the remaining salt and the turmeric.

Heat the oil in a large frying-pan. When it is hot, add the fish fillets and fry for 5 minutes on each side, or until they flake easily. Remove from the pan and drain on kitchen towels. Transfer to a warmed serving dish.

Pour over the reserved marinade and serve at once.

Serves 4

Preparation and cooking time: 1½ hours

TAMARIND FISH

Metric/Imperial	American
25g./1oz. tamarind	2 Tbs. tamarind
125ml./4fl.oz. boiling water	½ cup boiling water
4 medium red mullets, cleaned and with the eyes removed	4 medium red mullets, cleaned and with the eyes removed
50ml./2fl.oz. peanut oil	¼ cup peanut oil
4 red chillis, seeded	4 red chillis, seeded
1 medium onion, quartered	1 medium onion, quartered
2 garlic cloves	2 garlic cloves
1cm./½in. piece of fresh root ginger, peeled and sliced	½ piece of fresh green ginger, peeled and sliced
175ml./6fl.oz. water	¾ cup water
1 tsp. soya sauce	1 tsp. soy sauce
½ tsp. salt	½ tsp. salt

Put the tamarind into a bowl and pour over the water. Set aside until it is cool. Pour the contents of the bowl through a strainer into a bowl, pressing as much of the pulp through as possible. Rub the fish all over with the tamarind pulp and set aside.

Heat the oil in a large frying-pan. When it is hot, add the fish and cook for 7 minutes on each side.

Meanwhile, put the chillis, onion, garlic, ginger and 50ml./2fl.oz. (¼ cup) of water in a blender and blend to a smooth purée. Transfer the mixture to a small bowl and set aside.

Remove the fish from the pan and keep them hot. Add the spice purée to the pan and cook for 2 minutes, stirring constantly. Stir in the soy sauce, salt and remaining water and bring to the boil, stirring constantly. Reduce the heat to moderately low and return the fish to the pan, basting with the pan mixture.

Transfer the fish to a warmed serving dish and pour the sauce into a warmed sauceboat. Serve at once, with the fish.

Serves 4
Preparation and cooking time: 1 hour

IKAN BALI

(Balinese Sweet and Sour Fish)   (Indonesia)

The fish in this dish can be as you prefer – whole (but with the head and tail removed), in fillets, or in steaks. Slightly oily fish would be best – mackerel, mullet, or halibut steaks if you are feeling rich!

Metric/Imperial	American
1 Tbs. tamarind	1 Tbs. tamarind
50ml./2fl.oz. boiling water	¼ cup boiling water
3 Tbs. peanut oil	3 Tbs. peanut oil
1 large onion, finely chopped	1 large onion, finely chopped
2 garlic cloves, crushed	2 garlic cloves, crushed
4cm./1½in. piece of fresh root ginger, peeled and chopped	1½in. piece of fresh green ginger, peeled and chopped
1 tsp. chopped lemon grass or grated lemon rind	1 tsp. chopped lemon grass or grated lemon rind

Metric/Imperial	American
½ tsp. laos powder (optional)	½ tsp. laos powder (optional)
1 tsp. dried red chillis or sambal ulek	1 tsp. dried red chillis or sambal ulek
1½ Tbs. soya sauce	1 Tbs. soy sauce
1½ Tbs. lemon juice	1½ Tbs. lemon juice
1 Tbs. soft brown sugar	1 Tbs. soft brown sugar
vegetable oil for deep-frying	vegetable oil for deep-frying
700g./1½lb. fish	1½lb. fish
50g./2oz. cornflour	½ cup cornstarch

Put the tamarind into a bowl and pour over the boiling water. Set aside until it is cool. Pour the contents of the bowl through a strainer into a second bowl, pressing as much of the pulp through as possible. Set aside.

Heat the peanut oil in a small saucepan. When it is hot, add the onion, garlic and ginger and stir-fry for 3 minutes. Stir in the lemon grass or rind, laos powder and chillis or sambal ulek and continue to stir-fry for a further 2 minutes. Add the soy sauce, lemon juice, sugar and tamarind liquid and cook, stirring constantly until the sugar has dissolved. Remove the pan from the heat and set aside. Keep hot.

Fill a large deep-frying pan about one-third full with vegetable oil and heat until the oil is hot. Gently coat the fish in the cornflour, shaking off any excess, then carefully lower into the oil. Cook for 3 to 8 minutes (depending on the type of fish and cut used), or until crisp and golden brown. Remove the fish from the oil and drain on kitchen towels.

Return the saucepan containing the sauce to low heat and heat gently until it is hot. Arrange the fish on a warmed serving dish and spoon over the sauce. Serve at once.
Serves 4-6
Preparation and cooking time: 30 minutes

GULEH IKAN

(Fish Curry)   (Malaysia)

Metric/Imperial	American
1 large onion, chopped	1 large onion, chopped
1 garlic clove	1 garlic clove
2½cm./1in. piece of fresh root ginger, peeled and chopped	1in. piece of fresh green ginger, peeled and chopped
2 chillis, chopped	2 chillis, chopped
250ml./8fl.oz. thin coconut milk	1 cup thin coconut milk
1 Tbs. ground coriander	1 Tbs. ground coriander
½ tsp. ground cumin	½ tsp. ground cumin
½ tsp. turmeric	½ tsp. turmeric
½ tsp. ground fennel	½ tsp. ground fennel
1 tsp. chopped lemon grass or grated lemon rind	1 tsp. chopped lemon grass or grated lemon rind
125ml./4fl.oz. thick coconut milk	½ cup thick coconut milk
1 Tbs. tamarind	1 Tbs. tamarind
50ml./2fl.oz. boiling water	¼ cup boiling water
½kg./1lb. firm white fish steaks (cod, grey mullet, etc.), chopped	1lb. firm white fish steaks (cod, grey mullet, etc.), chopped

Put the onion, garlic, ginger and chillis into a blender and blend to a purée (add a spoonful or two of thin coconut milk if the mixture is too dry). Transfer the mixture to a saucepan and stir in half the thin coconut milk and the spices and lemon grass or rind.

Set the saucepan over moderate heat and add the remaining thin coconut milk and the thick coconut milk. Bring to the boil, reduce the heat to low and simmer for 15 minutes.

Meanwhile, put the tamarind into a bowl and pour over the boiling water. Set aside until it is cool. Pour the contents of the bowl through a strainer into the saucepan, pressing as much of the pulp through as possible.

Stir in the fish pieces and bring to the boil again. Reduce the heat to low and simmer for 10 to 15 minutes, or until the flesh flakes easily. Serve at once.
Serves 3–4
Preparation and cooking time : 50 minutes

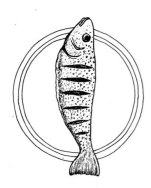

PLA PRIO WAN

(Fried Fish with Piquant Sauce)   (Thailand)

Any whole fish suitable for frying can be used in this dish; sea bream is probably the best but red snapper and jewfish could also be used.

Metric/Imperial	American
1 x 1kg./2lb. whole fish, cleaned, gutted and with the head still on	1 x 2lb. whole fish, cleaned, gutted and with the head still on
25g./1oz. cornflour	¼ cup cornstarch
vegetable oil for deep-frying	vegetable oil for deep-frying
1 Tbs. chopped coriander leaves	1 Tbs. chopped coriander leaves
PIQUANT SAUCE	PIQUANT SAUCE
1 Tbs. peanut oil	1 Tbs. peanut oil
10cm./4in. piece of fresh root ginger, peeled and finely chopped	4in. piece of fresh green ginger, peeled and finely chopped
1 garlic clove, crushed	1 garlic clove, crushed
1 red chilli, seeded and chopped	1 red chilli, seeded and chopped
4 Tbs. wine vinegar	4 Tbs. wine vinegar
4 Tbs. soft brown sugar	4 Tbs. soft brown sugar
125ml./4fl.oz. water	½ cup water
3 spring onions, green part included, finely chopped	3 scallions, green part included, finely chopped
1 Tbs. soya sauce	1 Tbs. soy sauce
1 Tbs. cornflour, mixed to a paste with 1 Tbs. water	1 Tbs. cornstarch, mixed to a paste with 1 Tbs. water

Rub the fish, inside and out, with salt, then wash and dry on kitchen towels. Make four or five deep incisions on each side of the fish, almost to the centre bone. Coat the fish in the cornflour (cornstarch) shaking off any excess.

Fill a large deep-frying pan one-third full with oil and heat it until it is very hot. Carefully lower the fish into the pan and deep-fry it for 5 minutes, or until it is golden brown and crisp. Remove the fish from the oil and drain on kitchen towels. Keep hot while you make the sauce.

Heat the oil in a deep frying-pan. When it is hot, add the ginger and garlic and stir-fry for 2 minutes. Stir in all the remaining sauce ingredients, except the cornflour (cornstarch) and bring to the boil, stirring constantly. Reduce the heat to moderately low and cook for 3 minutes. Stir in the cornflour (cornstarch) mixture and continue to cook the sauce until it thickens and becomes translucent.

Arrange the fish on a warmed serving dish and pour over the sauce. Garnish with the coriander and serve at once.
Serves 4–6
Preparation and cooking time : 35 minutes

SHELL FOOD

PRAWNS IN CHILLI SAUCE

(Singapore)

Metric/Imperial	American
4 Tbs. peanut oil	4 Tbs. peanut oil
½kg./1lb. shelled prawns	1lb. shelled shrimp
1 garlic clove, crushed	1 garlic clove, crushed
4cm./1½in. piece of fresh root ginger, peeled and chopped	1½in. piece of fresh green ginger, peeled and chopped
2 red chillis, chopped	2 red chillis, chopped
1 green pepper, pith and seeds removed and cut into strips	1 green pepper, pith and seeds removed and cut into strips
1 Tbs. Chinese chilli sauce	1 Tbs. Chinese chilli sauce
1 Tbs. tomato purée	1 Tbs. tomato paste
salt and pepper	salt and pepper
2 spring onions, chopped	2 scallions, chopped

Heat the oil in a large, deep frying-pan. When it is hot, add the prawns (shrimp) and stir-fry for 5 minutes, or until they are cooked. Using a slotted spoon, transfer the prawns (shrimp) to a plate. Keep hot.

Add the garlic, ginger, chillis and pepper to the pan and stir-fry for 3 minutes. Stir in the chilli sauce, tomato purée (paste) and seasoning to taste and stir-fry for a further 2 minutes. Return the prawns (shrimp) to the pan and stir-fry for 1 minute, or until they are well blended with the sauce.

Transfer to a warmed serving bowl and sprinkle over the spring onions (scallions). Serve at once.

Serves 4–6
Preparation and cooking time: 25 minutes

CHILLI CRAB

(Singapore)

Metric/Imperial	American
vegetable oil for deep-frying	vegetable oil for deep-frying
3 medium crabs, claws cracked and chopped through the shell into pieces	3 medium crabs, claws cracked and chopped through the shell into pieces
3 red chillis, chopped	3 red chillis, chopped
1cm./½in. piece of fresh root ginger, peeled and chopped	½in. piece of fresh green ginger, peeled and chopped
2 garlic cloves, crushed	2 garlic cloves, crushed
2 tsp. sugar	2 tsp. sugar
salt and pepper	salt and pepper
250ml./8fl.oz. chicken stock	1 cup chicken stock
2 tsp. cornflour, mixed to a paste with 2 tsp. water	2 tsp. cornstarch, mixed to a paste with 2 tsp. water
1 egg, lightly beaten	1 egg, lightly beaten
1 tsp. vinegar	1 tsp. vinegar
2 Tbs. tomato purée	2 Tbs. tomato paste

Fill a large deep-frying pan one-third full with oil and heat it until it is very hot. Carefully lower the crab pieces, a few at a time, into the oil and deep-fry for 1 minute. Using tongs or a slotted spoon, remove the pieces from the oil and drain on kitchen towels.

Reserve 3 tablespoons of the oil from the pan and pour it into a deep frying-pan. When it is hot, add the chillis, ginger and garlic. Fry, stirring occasionally, for 3 minutes. Return the crab pieces to the pan and add sugar, salt and pepper to taste, and stock. Bring to the boil, reduce the heat to low and cover the pan. Simmer for 15 minutes, or until the crab pieces are cooked through. Stir in the cornflour (cornstarch) mixture and cook until the liquid thickens and becomes translucent.

Stir in all of the remaining ingredients and cook gently for 2 to 3 minutes, or until the egg 'sets'.

Transfer the mixture to a large warmed serving bowl or deep serving platter and serve at once.

Serves 4
Preparation and cooking time: 1 hour

KARI BONGKONG LASAK

(Curried Shrimps and Cucumbers)   (Cambodia)

Metric/Imperial	American
2 garlic cloves, crushed	2 garlic cloves, crushed
2 spring onions, chopped	2 scallions, chopped
4cm./1½in. piece of fresh root ginger, peeled and chopped	1½in. piece of fresh green ginger, peeled and chopped
1 tsp. ground fennel	1 tsp. ground fennel
2 tsp. ground coriander	2 tsp. ground coriander
½ tsp. turmeric	½ tsp. turmeric
2 tsp. hot chilli powder	2 tsp. hot chilli powder
4 Tbs. peanut oil	4 Tbs. peanut oil
½kg./1lb. shelled prawns	1lb. shelled shrimp
450ml./15fl.oz. coconut milk	2 cups coconut milk
1 cucumber, quartered lengthways, seeds removed and cut into thick slices	1 cucumber, quartered lengthways, seeds removed and cut into thick slices
2 tsp. chopped lemon grass or grated lemon rind	2 tsp. chopped lemon grass or grated lemon rind
juice of 1 lemon	juice of 1 lemon
1 tsp. sugar	1 tsp. sugar
1 Tbs. fish sauce	1 Tbs. fish sauce

Put the garlic, spring onions (scallions) and ginger into a blender and blend to a purée. Scrape the mixture from the blender and transfer to a mixing bowl. Stir in the ground spices.

Heat the oil in a deep frying-pan. When it is hot, add the spice purée and stir-fry for 3 minutes. Add the prawns or shrimp and stir-fry for 5 minutes. Stir in the coconut milk and bring to the boil. Reduce the heat to low, add the cucumber and remaining ingredients and simmer gently for 5 minutes, or until the cucumber is translucent.

Serve at once.

Serves 6
Preparation and cooking time: 25 minutes

The cuisine of Cambodia tends to be overshadowed by its neigbours Vietnam and Thailand, but it has many unique features of its own. One of the most popular dishes is Kari Bongkong Lasak, a refreshing mixture of curried shrimps and cucumbers cooked in coconut milk flavoured with lemon.

TOM VO VIEN

(Shrimp Cakes)   (Vietnam)

Metric/Imperial	American
½kg./1lb. shelled prawns	1lb. shelled shrimp
1 Tbs. fish sauce	1 Tbs. fish sauce
½ tsp. sugar	½ tsp. sugar
2 spring onions, chopped	2 scallions, chopped
3 Tbs. chopped coriander leaves	3 Tbs. chopped coriander leaves
salt and pepper	salt and pepper
125ml./4fl.oz. peanut oil	½ cup peanut oil

Put the prawns or shrimp, fish sauce, sugar, spring onions (scallions), half the coriander leaves and seasoning into a blender and blend to a smooth paste. Shape into little cakes with floured hands and chill in the refrigerator for 15 minutes.

Cover the bottom of a frying-pan with half the oil. When it is hot, add about half the cakes and fry for 5 minutes on each side, or until they are golden and cooked through. Cook the remaining cakes in the same way. Drain on kitchen towels and serve hot, with nuoc cham (page 92).

Serves 4-6
Preparation and cooking time: 30 minutes

GULEH UDANG DENGAN LABU KUNING

(Prawn [Shrimp] and Marrow [Squash] Curry)   (Malaysia)

If you prefer, courgettes (zucchini) can be used instead of marrow (squash) in this recipe. If you do use them, do not peel – the green skin will make the dish look particularly attractive.

Metric/Imperial	American
1 large onion, chopped	1 large onion, chopped
2 red chillis, chopped	2 red chillis, chopped
1 tsp. chopped lemon grass or grated lemon rind	1 tsp. chopped lemon grass or grated lemon rind
1 tsp. turmeric	1 tsp. turmeric
¼ tsp. laos powder (optional)	¼ tsp. laos powder (optional)
½ tsp. dried basil	½ tsp. dried basil
250ml./8fl.oz. water	1 cup water
1 tsp. lemon juice	1 tsp. lemon juice
350g./12oz. marrow, peeled and cut into cubes	2 cups peeled and cubed winter squash
½kg./1lb. peeled prawns	1lb. peeled shrimp
175ml./6fl.oz. thick coconut milk	¾ cup thick coconut milk

Put the onion and chillis into a blender and blend to a smooth purée. Transfer the purée to a saucepan, then stir in the lemon grass or rind, turmeric, laos powder and basil until they are thoroughly blended. Gradually stir in the water and lemon juice.

Set the saucepan over moderately low heat and cook the mixture until it comes to the boil, stirring constantly. Reduce the heat to low and add the marrow (squash) cubes. Cook the mixture gently for 5 minutes, or until the cubes are half cooked. Add the prawns (shrimp) and coconut milk and continue to cook gently for a further 5 minutes, or until the prawns (shrimp) are cooked through and tender.

Transfer the mixture to a warmed serving bowl or large serving platter and serve at once.

Serves 4
Preparation and cooking time: 20 minutes

UKOY

(Shrimp and Sweet Potato Cakes)   (Philippines)

Metric/Imperial	American
10 medium shrimps, in the shell	10 medium shrimp, in the shell
300ml./10fl.oz. water	1¼ cups water
125g./4oz. plain flour	1 cup all-purpose flour
125g./4oz. cornflour	1 cup cornstarch
1 tsp. salt	1 tsp. salt
1 large egg, beaten	1 large egg, beaten
2 sweet potatoes, peeled	2 sweet potatoes, peeled
4 spring onions, chopped	4 scallions, chopped
salt and pepper	salt and pepper
vegetable oil for deep-frying	vegetable oil for deep-frying
DIPPING SAUCE	DIPPING SAUCE
2 garlic cloves, crushed	2 garlic cloves, crushed
1 tsp. salt	1 tsp. salt
125ml./4fl.oz. malt vinegar	½ cup cider vinegar

First make the dipping sauce. Stir the garlic and salt into the vinegar until all the ingredients are thoroughly combined. Set aside.

Put the shrimps and water into a small saucepan and bring to the boil. Cook for about 5 minutes, or until the shrimps are cooked through. Remove from the heat and transfer the shrimps to a plate. Strain the cooking liquid and reserve it. Remove the shells and veins from the shrimps.

Put the flour, cornflour (cornstarch) and salt into a mixing bowl. Gradually beat in the egg, then the reserved shrimp liquid until the mixture resembles a slightly thick pancake batter. Grate the sweet potatoes into the mixture, then stir until it is completely blended. Beat in the spring onions (scallions) and seasoning to taste.

Fill a large deep-frying pan about one-third full with oil and heat until it is hot. Carefully slide about a heaped tablespoonful of the batter mixture into the oil and arrange a shrimp in the centre. Cook the cakes in this way, two or three at a time, pressing down lightly on them with a slotted spoon and spooning oil over occasionally. Cook for about 3 minutes, then carefully turn over and cook for a further 3 minutes, or until the cakes are crisp and golden brown. Remove from the oil and drain on kitchen towels.

Serve at once, with the dipping sauce.

Makes 10 cakes
Preparation and cooking time: 50 minutes

Cabbage with Shrimps,
Penang-Style is a brilliant
example of the Oriental
ability to make a very little
go a long way. Here an
ordinary white cabbage is
transformed by the
addition of ginger and a
few shrimps. The result
can either be a vegetable
accompaniment dish, or a
light meal on its own. Or,
best of all, it can be served
in the Oriental way, as one
of several dishes arranged
all at once on the table.

VEGETABLES & ACCOMPANIMENTS

CABBAGE WITH SHRIMP

(Malaysia)

Metric/Imperial	American
3 Tbs. vegetable oil	3 Tbs. vegetable oil
225g./8oz. prawns, shelled	8oz. shrimp, shelled
2 medium onions, sliced	2 medium onions, sliced
4cm./1½in. piece of fresh root ginger, peeled and shredded	1½in. piece of fresh green ginger, peeled and shredded
2 red chillis, finely chopped	2 red chillis, finely chopped
1 medium white cabbage, shredded	1 medium white cabbage, shredded
1 tsp. salt	1 tsp. salt
1cm./½in. slice of creamed coconut, dissolved in 1½ Tbs. boiling water	½in. slice of creamed coconut, dissolved in 1½ Tbs. boiling water

Heat the oil in a large frying-pan. When it is hot, add the prawns or shrimp and fry for 3 to 5 minutes, or until they are pink and firm. Transfer to a plate and keep hot.

Add the onions, ginger and chillis to the pan and fry, stirring occasionally, until the onions are soft. Stir in the cabbage and stir-fry for 2 minutes. Stir in the salt and coconut mixture and cook for 5 minutes, stirring frequently. Stir in the prawns or shrimp. Serve at once.
Serves 6
Preparation and cooking time: 30 minutes

SAMBAL I

(Potato Sambal)   (Indonesia)

Metric/Imperial	American
225g./8oz. potatoes, boiled in their skins, peeled and coarsely mashed	8oz. potatoes, boiled in their skins, peeled and coarsely mashed
4 spring onions, finely chopped	4 scallions, finely chopped
2 green chillis, finely chopped	2 green chillis, finely chopped
½ tsp. salt	½ tsp. salt
1 Tbs. lemon juice	1 Tbs. lemon juice
2 Tbs. thick coconut milk	2 Tbs. thick coconut milk
1 Tbs. chopped coriander leaves	1 Tbs. chopped coriander leaves

Combine all the ingredients, except the coriander, in a shallow serving bowl. Taste the mixture and add more salt or lemon juice if necessary. Sprinkle over the coriander.

Chill in the refrigerator until ready to use.
Serves 3–4
Preparation and cooking time: 25 minutes

SAMBAL II

(Chicken Liver Sambal) (Indonesia)

Metric/Imperial	American
3 Tbs. vegetable oil	3 Tbs. vegetable oil
2 medium onions, very finely chopped	2 medium onions, very finely chopped
2 garlic cloves, crushed	2 garlic cloves, crushed
700g./1½lb. chicken livers, cleaned and halved	1½lb. chicken livers, cleaned and halved
2-4 red chillis, finely chopped	2-4 red chillis, finely chopped
1 tsp. chopped lemon grass or grated lemon rind	1 tsp. chopped lemon grass or grated lemon rind
½ tsp. laos powder	½ tsp. laos powder
1 tsp. sugar	1 tsp. sugar
1 tsp. salt	1 tsp. salt
2 curry leaves (optional)	2 curry leaves (optional)
350ml./12fl.oz. thick coconut milk	1½ cups thick coconut milk

Heat the oil in a large saucepan. When it is hot, add the onions and garlic and fry, stirring occasionally, until the onions are golden brown. Add the chicken livers and fry until they lose their pinkness. Stir in all the remaining ingredients and bring to the boil, stirring occasionally. Reduce the heat to low and simmer for 20 minutes, or until the sauce is thick.

Spoon the sambal into a warmed serving dish and serve at once.

Serves 4–6
Preparation and cooking time: 35 minutes

SAMBAL GORENG TELUR

(Egg and Chilli Sambal) (Indonesia)

Metric/Imperial	American
4 eggs	4 eggs
1 large onion, chopped	1 large onion, chopped
2 garlic cloves	2 garlic cloves
1 Tbs. dried chillis or sambal ulek	1 Tbs. dried chillis or sambal ulek
3 Tbs. peanut oil	3 Tbs. peanut oil
½ tsp. blachan (dried shrimp paste)	½ tsp. blachan (dried shrimp paste)
1 tsp. sugar	1 tsp. sugar
½ tsp. laos powder	½ tsp. laos powder
½ tsp. chopped lemon grass or grated lemon rind	½ tsp. chopped lemon grass or grated lemon rind
250ml./8fl.oz. coconut milk	1 cup coconut milk

Hard-boil the eggs, then shell and halve them. Set them aside. Put the onion, garlic and chillis into a blender and blend to a rough purée.

Heat the oil in a large, shallow saucepan. When it is hot, add the onion puree and fry, stirring frequently, for 2 minutes. Stir in the remaining ingredients and bring to the boil, stirring constantly. Reduce the heat to very low and carefully add the egg halves. Simmer gently until the mixture thickens slightly.

Serve at once.

Serves 6–8
Preparation and cooking time: 20 minutes

THAN THAT

(Cucumber Pickle)   (Burma)

Metric/Imperial	American
2 cucumbers, peeled and cut in half lengthways	2 cucumbers, peeled and cut in half lengthways
50ml./2fl.oz. vinegar	¼ cup vinegar
250ml./8fl.oz. water	1 cup water
Pepper and salt	Pepper and salt
75ml./3fl.oz. sesame oil	⅓ cup sesame oil
1 large onion, finely chopped	1 large onion, finely chopped
6 large garlic cloves, crushed	6 large garlic cloves, crushed
2 Tbs. sesame seeds	2 Tbs. sesame seeds

Remove the seeds from the cucumbers and cut into strips. Put into a saucepan and add all the vinegar except 1 tablespoon, the water and seasoning and bring to the boil. Reduce the heat to low and simmer for 5 minutes, or until the strips are translucent. Drain and transfer the strips to a shallow serving bowl to cool to room temperature.

Heat the oil in a frying-pan. When it is hot, add the onion and garlic and fry gently for 5 minutes, or until they are lightly browned. Transfer to a plate. Add the sesame seeds to the pan and fry gently until they are lightly toasted. Tip the sesame seeds and oil into the onion and garlic, add the reserved vinegar and mix. When the cucumber strips are cool, pour over the sesame oil mixture and toss gently. Serve at once.

Serves 6–8
Preparation and cooking time: 1 hour

ROJAK

(Mixed Salad)   (Malaysia)

Metric/Imperial	American
½ cucumber, diced	½ cucumber, diced
½ small pineapple, peeled, cored and diced	½ small pineapple, peeled, cored and diced
1 green mango, peeled, stoned and diced	1 green mango, peeled, pitted and diced
2 dried red chillis, crumbled	2 dried red chillis, crumbled
DRESSING	DRESSING
2 tsp. dried chillis or sambal ulek	2 tsp. dried chillis or sambal ulek
½ tsp. blachan (dried shrimp paste)	½ tsp. blachan (dried shrimp paste)
1 Tbs. sugar	1 Tbs. sugar
1 Tbs. vinegar	1 Tbs. vinegar
1 Tbs. lemon juice	1 Tbs. lemon juice

Put the cucumber, pineapple and mango in a shallow bowl. Combine all the dressing ingredients in a blender, then pour over the salad. Toss gently, then scatter over the crumbled chillis.

Set aside at room temperature for 10 minutes before serving.

Serves 6
Preparation and cooking time: 15 minutes

GADO-GADO

(Indonesia)

Metric/Imperial	American
½ small white cabbage, shredded	½ small white cabbage, shredded
225g./8oz. French beans	1⅓ cups green beans
125g./4oz. bean sprouts	½ cup bean sprouts
¼ small cucumber, chopped	¼ small cucumber, chopped
2 potatoes	2 potatoes
2 hard-boiled eggs, sliced	2 hard-boiled eggs, sliced
PEANUT SAUCE	PEANUT SAUCE
2 Tbs. peanut oil	2 Tbs. peanut oil
2 garlic cloves, crushed	2 garlic cloves, crushed
2 red chillis, crumbled	2 red chillis, crumbled
1 tsp. blachan (dried shrimp paste)	1 tsp. blachan (dried shrimp paste)
½ tsp. laos powder	½ tsp. laos powder
1 tsp. soft brown sugar	1 tsp. soft brown sugar
4 Tbs. peanut butter	4 Tbs. peanut butter
250ml./8fl.oz. coconut milk	1 cup coconut milk
2 tsp. lemon juice or vinegar	2 tsp. lemon juice or vinegar
GARNISH	GARNISH
prawn crackers	shrimp crackers
2 Tbs. chopped spring onions	2 Tbs. chopped scallions

Cook all of the vegetables lightly but separately. Drain and arrange in layers on a serving platter. Set aside until cold.

To make the sauce, heat the oil in a small saucepan. When it is hot, add the garlic and chillis and stir-fry for 3 minutes. Stir in the blachan, laos and sugar and cook until they have dissolved. Stir in the peanut butter and coconut milk and blend thoroughly. Bring to the boil. Remove from the heat and stir in the lemon juice or vinegar.

Pour the sauce over the top of the vegetables and garnish with the crackers and chopped spring onions (scallions).

Serves 6
Preparation and cooking time: 40 minutes

NUOC CHAM

(Prepared Fish Sauce) (Vietnam)

Metric/Imperial	American
4 Tbs. fish sauce	4 Tbs. fish sauce
2 garlic cloves, crushed	2 garlic cloves, crushed
juice of 1 lemon (use a little flesh as well)	juice of 1 lemon (use a little flesh as well)
½ dried chilli, crumbled (optional)	½ dried chilli, crumbled (optional)
1 tsp. sugar	1 tsp. sugar
2 Tbs. water	2 Tbs. water

Mix all the ingredients, except the water, together and beat well. Add the water and stir well. If you prefer the sauce less strong, dilute it with more water to taste.
Makes 1 table serving
Preparation time: 5 minutes

YAHM CHOMPU

(Savoury Fruit Salad)   (Thailand)

Metric/Imperial	American
1 large tart apple, diced	1 large tart apple, diced
1 small pineapple, peeled, sliced then diced	1 small pineapple, peeled, sliced then diced
225g./8oz. lean cooked pork, diced	1⅓ cups diced lean cooked pork
125g./4oz. prawns, shelled	4oz. shrimps, shelled
2 Tbs. chopped spring onions	2 Tbs. chopped scallions
1 cos lettuce, shredded	1 romaine lettuce, shredded
DRESSING	DRESSING
6 Tbs. olive oil	6 Tbs. olive oil
juice of 1 lemon	juice of 1 lemon
2 Tbs. soya sauce	2 Tbs. soy sauce
1 Tbs. soft brown sugar	1 Tbs. soft brown sugar

To make the dressing, combine all the ingredients in a small bowl and set aside.

Put the fruit, pork, prawns or shrimp and spring onions (scallions) in a large bowl. Pour over the dressing and mix well.

Arrange the lettuce around the edges of a dish and pile the salad into the centre. Serve at once.

Serves 6
Preparation time: 10 minutes

Fruit is often served as a salad, or is included in salads in South-East Asia, and Yahm Chompu from from Thailand is no exception. This particular version is made more substantial by the addition of pork and shrimps.

CHA GIO

(Vietnamese Spring Rolls)

In Vietnam, these rolls are wrapped in special rice paper called banh-da and then deep-fried; spring roll wrappers, however, are a good substitute. If you prefer, minced (ground) pork or shrimp may be substituted for the crab.

Metric/Imperial	American
225g./8oz. crabmeat, shell and cartilage removed and flaked	8oz. crabmeat, shell and cartilage removed and flaked
1 small onion, finely chopped	1 small onion, finely chopped
1 carrot, grated	1 carrot, grated
50g./2oz. bean sprouts	$\frac{1}{4}$ cup bean sprouts
1 egg	1 egg
10 spring roll wrappers	10 spring roll wrappers
vegetable oil for deep-frying	vegetable oil for deep-frying

Put the crabmeat, onion, carrot, bean sprouts, and egg in a bowl and combine thoroughly. Put about 2 tablespoons of the filling in the centre of one spring roll wrapper and carefully roll up diagonally to make a neat parcel, making sure that the filling is completely enclosed.

Fill a large deep-frying pan one-third full of oil and heat it until it is very hot. Carefully lower the rolls (on a spatula or slotted spoon), a few at a time, into the oil and fry until they are golden brown and crisp. Remove from the oil and drain on kitchen towels. Serve hot with nuoc cham (see recipe on page 92)
Serves 8
Preparation and cooking time: 20 minutes

MASAK LEMAK

(Cabbage Curry)   (Malaysia)

Metric/Imperial	American
1 onion, sliced	1 onion, sliced
2 red chillis, chopped	2 red chillis, chopped
$\frac{1}{2}$ tsp. blachan (dried shrimp paste)	$\frac{1}{2}$ tsp. blachan (dried shrimp paste)
1 tsp. turmeric	1 tsp. turmeric
250ml./8fl.oz. thin coconut milk	1 cup thin coconut milk
1 potato, cut into large cubes	1 potato, cut into large cubes
1 small white cabbage, shredded	1 small white cabbage, shredded
125ml./4fl.oz. thick coconut milk	$\frac{1}{2}$ cup thick coconut milk

Put the onion, chillis, blachan, turmeric and thin coconut milk into a saucepan. Bring to the boil. Reduce the heat to moderately low and add the potato pieces. Cook for 10 minutes, or until the potato is half-cooked. Stir in the cabbage and cook for 5 minutes. Pour over the remaining thick coconut milk and bring to the boil, stirring constantly.

Serve at once.
Serves 4
Preparation and cooking time: 30 minutes

URAP

(Mixed Vegetables with Coconut) (Indonesia)

Metric/Imperial	American
2 celery stalks, cut into 2½cm./1in. lengths	2 celery stalks, cut into 1in. lengths
225g./8oz. bean sprouts	1 cup bean sprouts
225g./8oz. French beans, cut into 2½cm./1in. lengths	1⅓ cups green beans, cut into 1in. lengths
125g./4oz. Chinese cabbage, shredded	1 cup shredded Chinese cabbage
½ fresh coconut, grated	½ fresh coconut, grated
2 spring onions, finely chopped	2 scallions, finely chopped
1 tsp. sambal ulek or 2 dried red chillis, crumbled	1 tsp. sambal ulek or 2 dried red chillis, crumbled
½ tsp. blachan (dried shrimp paste)	½ tsp. blachan (dried shrimp paste)
1 Tbs. lemon juice	1 Tbs. lemon juice

Steam or boil the vegetables, separately, until they are just cooked through. Set aside and keep hot.

Combine all the remaining ingredients in a mixing bowl until they are well blended. Stir into the vegetables until all the vegetable pieces are coated.

Serve at once, either as a vegetable dish or as an accompaniment.

Serves 6
Preparation and cooking time: 15 minutes

SERUNDENG

(Coconut and Peanut Garnish) (Indonesia)

Metric/Imperial	American
1 Tbs. peanut oil	1 Tbs. peanut oil
1 small onion, chopped	1 small onion, chopped
1 garlic clove, crushed	1 garlic clove, crushed
1 tsp. blachan (dried shrimp paste)	1 tsp. blachan (dried shrimp paste)
1 Tbs. ground coriander	1 Tbs. ground coriander
2 Tbs. sugar	2 Tbs. sugar
1 tsp. salt	1 tsp. salt
125g./4oz. coconut, freshly grated	1 cup freshly grated coconut
225g./8oz. shelled salted peanuts	1⅓ cups shelled salted peanuts

Heat the oil in a saucepan. When it is hot, add the onion and garlic and fry, stirring occasionally, until the onion is soft. Stir in the blachan and cook for 5 minutes, stirring frequently. Reduce the heat to low. Stir in the coriander, sugar, salt and coconut and fry, stirring constantly, until the coconut is golden brown. Stir in the salted peanuts and mix until the ingredients are thoroughly blended.

Remove from the heat. Set aside to cool completely, then transfer the serundeng to a storage jar. Store in a cool, dry place until you are ready to use.

Serves 6–8
Preparation and cooking time: 25 minutes

Kachang Bendi Goreng is a Malaysian dish of fried mixed green vegetables with shrimps. It can be served as part of an Oriental meal, as a fairly substantial vegetable accompaniment, or even as a light snack dish on its own.

KACHANG BENDI GORENG

(Fried Mixed Green Vegetables with Shrimps)   (Malaysia)

Metric/Imperial	American
3 Tbs. peanut oil	3 Tbs. peanut oil
2 onions, finely chopped	2 onions, finely chopped
1 garlic clove, crushed	1 garlic clove, crushed
2 green chillis, finely chopped	2 green chillis, finely chopped
4cm./1½in. piece of fresh root ginger, peeled and chopped	1½in. piece of fresh green ginger, peeled and chopped
1 Tbs. ground almonds	1 Tbs. ground almonds
2 Tbs. soya sauce	2 Tbs. soy sauce
½ tsp. black pepper	½ tsp. black pepper
350g./12oz. prawns, shelled	12 oz. shrimp, shelled
1 green pepper, pith and seeds removed and sliced	1 green pepper, pith and seeds removed and sliced
175g./6oz. French beans	1 cup green beans
2 courgettes, sliced	2 zucchini, sliced

Heat the oil in a large frying-pan. When it is hot, add the onions, garlic, chillis and ginger and fry, stirring occasionally, until the onions are golden brown. Stir in the ground almonds, soy sauce and pepper and cook for 2 minutes. Add the prawns or shrimp and stir-fry for 3 minutes. Add the vegetables. Reduce the heat to low and simmer the mixture for 10 minutes, or until the vegetables are cooked through.

Serve at once.

Serves 6–8

Preparation and cooking time: 30 minutes

SAJUR LODEH

(Mixed Vegetables Cooked with Coconut)   (Indonesia)

Almost any vegetable can be used in this soupy dish although, traditionally, there would be a mixture of at least three or four different types. Chinese or white cabbage, courgettes (zucchini) or pumpkin, French (green) beans, bamboo shoots, aubergine (eggplant), onion or even leeks, would all be successful.

Metric/Imperial	American
1 medium onion, chopped	1 medium onion, chopped
2 garlic cloves, crushed	2 garlic cloves, crushed
1½ tsp. dried chillis or sambal ulek	1½ tsp. dried chillis or sambal ulek
1 tsp. blachan (dried shrimp paste)	1 tsp. blachan (dried shrimp paste)
½ tsp. laos powder	½ tsp. laos powder
3 Tbs. peanut oil	3 Tbs. peanut oil
700g./1½lb. mixed vegetables, cut into bite-sized pieces	1½lb. mixed vegetables, cut into bite-sized pieces
1 large tomato, blanched, peeled and chopped	1 large tomato, blanched, peeled and chopped
725ml./1¼ pints coconut milk	3 cups coconut milk
1 tsp. soft brown sugar	1 tsp. soft brown sugar
1 Tbs. peanut butter (optional)	1 Tbs. peanut butter (optional)

Put the onion, garlic, sambal ulek and blachan into a mortar and pound to a paste with a pestle. Alternatively, purée in a blender. Stir in the laos powder.

Heat the oil in a large saucepan. When it is very hot, add the spice paste and stir-fry for 2 minutes. Add the tomato and stir-fry for 3 minutes, or until it has pulped. Gradually stir in the coconut milk and bring to the boil. Add the veget-

ables to the pan, in the order in which they should be cooked (longest cooking vegetable first). Reduce the heat to moderately low and cook until they are just tender but still crisp. Stir in the sugar and peanut butter and simmer for 1 minute longer.

Transfer to a warmed serving bowl and serve at once.

Serves 6
Preparation and cooking time: 30 minutes

BAKED BANANAS

(Malaysia)

Metric/Imperial	American
50g./2oz. butter	4 Tbs. butter
50g./2oz. soft brown sugar	$\frac{1}{3}$ cup soft brown sugar
$\frac{1}{4}$ tsp. ground cloves	$\frac{1}{4}$ tsp. ground cloves
2 Tbs. orange juice	2 Tbs. orange juice
1 tsp. lemon juice	1 tsp. lemon juice
2$\frac{1}{2}$cm./1in. piece of fresh	1in. piece of fresh green
root ginger, peeled and finely diced	ginger, peeled and finely diced
6 bananas, sliced in half lengthways	6 bananas, sliced in half lengthways

Preheat the oven to fairly hot 190°C (Gas Mark 5, 375°F).

Cream the butter and sugar together until they are pale and soft. Beat in the cloves, orange and lemon juice and ginger.

Lay the bananas on a well-greased medium baking dish and spread the butter mixture over them. Put the dish into the oven and bake for 10 to 15 minutes, or until the top is bubbling and the bananas are cooked through and tender.

Remove from the oven and serve at once.

Serves 6
Preparation and cooking time: 30 minutes

One of the very best of the traditional rijsttafel accompaniments, Baked Bananas have the refreshing tang of oranges and lemons to counteract the slightly dense taste of the bananas.

GLOSSARY

Ajar
An Indian-style pickle, very popular throughout Malaysia and Indonesia. It is closely related to the Indian *achar*.

Annatto
Small red seeds used for flavouring throughout Latin America and in the Philippines. Obtainable from Latin American stores or better supermarkets. If unobtainable use a blend of paprika with a dash of turmeric for the same colouring effect. No flavouring substitute.

Blachan
A form of dried shrimp paste used extensively as a flavouring all over South-East Asia. It has a variety of names depending on its origin – in Malaysia, for instance, it is called *trasi* and in Thailand *kapi*. For ease of reference in this book it is always referred to as blachan (dried shrimp paste). Sold in plastic bags, in dry cakes or slabs, or even in cans. When opened always store in a covered container – as much to keep in the very strong taste as to keep it fresh! Keeps indefinitely. Available in oriental, especially Indonesian, stores.

Candle nuts
A hard, oily nut used extensively in Malay and Indonesian cooking, especially in curries. Virtually unobtainable in the West, so substitute brazil nuts, or even unsalted peanuts if necessary.

Coconut milk
The milk of the coconut fruit is a popular cooking gravy throughout the Orient. If fresh coconut milk is unavailable, make your own using 75g./3oz. creamed coconut slice and about 450ml./15fl.oz. (2 cups) of boiling water. Stir or blend until the liquid is white and has thickened. Increase the amount of coconut to make thick coconut milk, decrease slightly to make thin. If creamed coconut is not available, desiccated (shredded) coconut in the same quantities can be used instead.

Coriander
Many parts of the coriander plant are used in oriental cooking – the seeds and a ground version of the seeds are used in curries, and the leaves are used extensively as a garnish in all types of dishes; in Thailand and Burma coriander leaves are sprinkled over practically everything! Since it is a member of the parsley plant, chopped parsley can be used as a substitute, although the taste will not be nearly so pungent. Available from Indian, Greek and Mexican stores.

Daun pandan
Long, green leaves which are used as a flavouring all over Malaysia and Indonesia. The leaves are crushed and boiled before using. Virtually unobtainable in the West and no substitute. Omit if unavailable.

Fish sauce
A thin, brownish liquid made from fermented dried shrimp paste and used with great enthusiasm in many parts of South-East Asia. Thailand, Vietnam, Burma and Cambodia all have their versions – the Vietnamese, in fact, use it as a garnish in much the same way as the Chinese use soy sauce and Westerners would use salt and pepper. When used in cooking, it should be measured straight from the bottle; when used as a dipping sauce or condiment, it is usually diluted with water to which lemon juice and flesh has been added – and perhaps garlic too (see recipe for *nuoc cham*). Available from most Chinese stores, or other oriental stores and from any shop stocking Vietnamese specialities. If unavailable, an acceptable substitute can be provided by mixing equal portions of anchovy paste and light soy sauce together.

Jaggery
The raw sugar of the palm tree, used in curried dishes throughout the Orient. Available from Indian or other oriental stores. If unobtainable, substitute the unrefined dark sugar available in health food stores, or refined dark brown sugar.

Kapi
See under blachan

Kha
See under laos

Laos
A fragrant spice made from the tuberous galingal plant, which is somewhat similar in flavour to ginger, although more delicate. Found throughout South-East Asia but known by different names in each country. Laos is the Indonesian name; in Malaysia it is called *lengkuas*, in Thailand *kha*. For ease of reference, in this book, it is always referred to as laos powder. Obtainable from Indonesian stores and some better spice chains.

Lemon grass	A citron-smelling, bulbous plant somewhat similar in appearance to a small spring onion (scallion). A popular seasoning in South-East Asia, lemon grass is known as *serai* in Malaysia, *sereh* in Indonesia and is also found in Thai and Burmese cooking. For ease of reference, in this book it is always referred to as lemon grass. Sold fresh and in powdered form from Indonesian or oriental stores, but if unavailable in any form, then grated lemon rind can be substituted.
Lengkuas	See under laos
Lotus seeds	Small, fresh-tasting seeds used both in cooking and as a digestive in South-East Asia. Virtually unavailable in the West. No substitute.
Peanuts	Widely used as a garnish in Indonesian cooking and forms the basis of the famous *sate* sauce, used as an accompaniment to pork or chicken kebabs or *sate*. In this latter case, usually roasted then ground and mixed with the other sauce ingredients. To cut out some of the work, an acceptable short-cut is to use crunchy peanut butter for *sate* sauces.
Rambutan	An exotic oriental fruit, often eaten as a dessert. Available throughout Indonesia, Malaysia and Thailand. Virtually unobtainable in the West, though lychees make a near substitute.
Rijsttafel	Literally, rice table in Dutch, and in reality a series of contrasting and complementary dishes served together to make a complete Indonesian meal. The centre is always rice but the other dishes can range from six or eight up to thirty or forty, depending on the grandness of the occasion (and the quantity of the servings). Usually contains at least one *sate* dish with sauce, several different meat dishes (at least one curried), a fish dish, some pickle or sambal dishes and of course the garnish dishes of peanuts and *serundeng*, a mixture of ground peanuts and grated coconut (see recipe). A fuller description of rijsttafel is given in the introduction.
Serai or serah	See under lemon grass
Sambal ulek	A pungent mixture of ground red chillis and salt used both in cooking and as a condiment in Indonesian cooking. Available in jars or cans from better oriental or any Indonesian store. If unavailable commercially, substitute dried red chillis or make your own paste by grinding red chillis and salt to taste, then adding water until it forms a thick purée.
Tamarind	Acid-tasting seeded fruit. Tamarind is sold in thick slabs, usually dried, in Indian and other oriental stores. The juice from the pulp is used more often in recipes than the dried flesh itself. To make tamarind juice, put the tamarind into a bowl and pour over boiling water. Set aside until cool. Pour the contents of the bowl through a strainer and press through as much pulp as possible. It is now ready to use.
Trasi	See under blachan

RECIPE INDEX